# EARLY SOURCES OF THE LITURGY

Compiled and edited by

## LUCIEN DEISS, C.S.Sp.

*Translated by*
*Benet Weatherhead*

## GEOFFREY CHAPMAN
LONDON DUBLIN MELBOURNE 1967

Geoffrey Chapman Ltd,
18 High Street, Wimbledon, S.W. 19

Geoffrey Chapman (Ireland) Ltd,
5–7 Main Street, Blackrock, Co Dublin, Ireland

Geoffrey Chapman Pty Ltd,
459 Little Collins Street, Melbourne, Victoria

First published as *Aux sources de la liturgie* by
Editions Fleurus, 1963

Nihil obstat: R. D. Jacobus P. Wroe, D.D., Ph. D.,
censor deputatus

Imprimatur: H. Gibney,
vicarius generalis

Datum Southwarci die 23a Novembris 1966

Set in Monotype Garamond

*Made and printed in the Republic of Ireland by Cahill & Co, Limited, Parkgate St, Dublin 8*

# EARLY SOURCES OF THE LITURGY

# Table of Contents

# Introduction

*"To return in mind and heart to the sources of the liturgy."*
Pius XII

The collection, *Early Sources of the Liturgy*, presents the principal texts concerning the primitive liturgy from its origins to the fourth and fifth centuries.

The following are the sources which we have at our disposal at the present time from which to discover this liturgy:

— The narrative of the institution of the Lord's Supper according to the three-fold synoptic tradition and the First Epistle to the Corinthians. This narrative is at the centre of all celebrations of the Eucharist.

— The eucharistic prayer, that is, the prayer of thanksgiving, from the *Didache*. This prayer, with the blessing of bread and wine and the final thanksgiving, may very well have served as the framework of a Christian meal which in all probability included the sacrament of the Eucharist. It was to be taken up again in part in the anaphoras of Serapion of Thmuis and of Der Balyzeh.

— The witness of St Justin who, in his *First Apology*, describes the rites of baptism and the Eucharist as well as the celebration of the Lord's Day. This document goes back to the middle of the second century, about 150 A.D.

— The *Apostolic Tradition* of Hippolytus of Rome. This document, which was put together about 215 A.D., is of exceptional importance since it informs us of the state of liturgy and of Christian practice in the Church of Rome at the beginning of the third century.

— The *Didascalia of the Apostles*, which also dates from the beginning of the third century and is of Syrian origin.

— The *Euchology of Serapion of Thmuis*, put together about 350 A.D. in Egypt.

From the fourth century onwards the witnesses become more numerous but are of unequal value. They can be divided into two groups.

The first group comprises liturgical texts and collections. These works are for the most part anonymous and it is in fact a difficult matter to date them. Interpreting them too is full of snares and surprises. What has happened is that in the manuscript tradition in which they have come down to us heterogeneous elements have been superimposed on them from time to time—to such a point that it is only with difficulty and by relying on often risky hypotheses that scholars can arrive at the restoration of their primitive state. Conversely it can happen that they furnish us with very ancient formulas, going back well beyond the epoch in which they were put together.

We can include in this first group:

— The *Anaphora of Addai and Mari* which dates from the third century according to Botte or according to Raes from the fifth.

— The *Strasburg Papyrus* which goes back to the fourth century and represents the so-called liturgy of St Mark.

— The *Apostolic Constitutions* (fourth century) which used as sources the *Didascalia of the Apostles* (books 1 to 6), the *Didache* (book 7) and the *Apostolic Tradition* (book 8). This is the most considerable of the liturgical collections.

— The *Testament of Our Lord Jesus Christ*,[1] a writing whose eccentricity verges at times on extravagance, as the title itself might lead one to suppose. This work saw the light of day in the second half of the fifth century, probably among Monophysite circles in Syria.

— The *Euchology* of Der Balyzeh, rescued from the sands of

---

[1] Text in J. E. Rahmani, *Test. Domini nostri Jesu Christi*, Mainz, 1899.

Egypt. Despite the fact that it was put together fairly late (fifth/sixth century), it seems that the prayers which it contains can lay claim to a much greater antiquity.

The second group comprises writings which are based on liturgical texts and rites either to explain them or to draw moral exhortations from them. These commentaries, destined in the first place for contemporaries, are of the greatest interest for our own understanding of ancient liturgy. This group includes:

— *The Catechetical Instructions of St Cyril of Jerusalem*[1] which were delivered about the year 347. To these are usually added the *Mystagogical Catecheses*, though their authenticity is somewhat suspect and it is possible that they date from the 400s.

— The *Baptismal Catecheses* of St John Chrysostom discovered recently by A. Wenger (4 October, 1955).[2] These were delivered between 386 and 398 A.D.

— The treatises *On the Sacraments* and *On the Mysteries* of St Ambrose.[3] Here we have a series of catechetical instructions meant for the newly-baptized; they were delivered about 390 and taken down in shorthand by someone who was present.

— The Voyage of Etheria[4] in which the liturgy of Jerusalem is described as Etheria saw it during her pilgrimage to the Holy Places about the year 400.

— The *Catechetical Instructions* of Theodore of Mopsuestia (†428) in Cilicia.[5]

---

[1] *P.G.* 33, 331–1128.

[2] A. Wenger, *Jean Chrysostome. Huit Catéchèses baptismales* (Sources chrétiennes, 50), Paris, 1957.

[3] *On the Sacraments*, P.L. 16, 417–462. *On the Mysteries*, P.L. 16, 389–410. See also B. Botte, *Des sacrements. Des mystères* (Sources chrétiennes, 25b), Paris, 1961.

[4] *Corpus Christianorum Series Latina*, CLXXV, 1958. See also H. Pétré, *Éthérie. Journal de voyage* (Sources chrétiennes, 21), Paris, 1948.

[5] R. Tonneau and R. Devreesse, *Les Homélies catéchétiques de Théodore de Mopsueste* (Studi e testi, CXLV), Vatican City, 1949. See also Ruecker, *Ritus baptismi et missae quem descripsit Theodorus . . . in linguam latinam translatus*, Munich, 1933.

From these texts concerning the liturgy, the present collection makes use of the following:

— The narrative of the Institution of the Lord's Supper, according to the synoptic tradition and the First Epistle to the Corinthians (pp. 6–7).

— The eucharistic prayer from the *Didache* (pp. 11–16).

— The witness of St Justin in his *First Apology* (pp. 17–26).

— The *Apostolic Tradition* of Hippolytus of Rome (pp. 27–73).

— The *Didascalia of the Apostles* (pp. 75–96).

— The *Euchology of Serapion of Thmuis* (pp. 97–134).

— The *Anaphora of Addai and Mari* (pp. 135–140).

— The *Strasburg papyrus* (pp. 143–147).

— The *Apostolic Constitutions* (pp. 149–183).

— The *Euchology* of Der Balyzeh (pp. 185–194).

---

In the Encyclical *Mediator Dei* Pius XII wrote: "To return in mind and heart to the well-springs of the sacred liturgy is wise and praiseworthy, for the study of this subject, searching back to its origins, is of considerable use in helping us to penetrate more deeply and more carefully into the significance of festival-days, the meaning of the sacred ceremonies and of the formulas we use."[1]

We have the great good fortune to be living through the liturgical renewal of the present day. I hope that this return to

---

[1] *Mediator Dei*, 20 November, 1947.

"the well-springs of the liturgy" will restore a relish for penetrating further into the spiritual significance of the rites by which we are made holy, and perhaps also the desire to make use, in our own prayer to the Lord, of these forms hammered out by the devotion of the first centuries.

# I

# The Passover Meal and the Institution of the Eucharist in the New Testament

# The last Passover meal of Jesus according to the narrative of Luke 22, 15-18

15    And Jesus said to his disciples:
"I have longed and longed
to eat this Passover with you
before I suffer.

16    For I tell you:
From now on, I shall not eat it again
until it is fulfilled,
in the kingdom of God."

17    And taking a cup,
he gave thanks and said:
"Take this
and share it among you.

18    For I tell you:
From now on I shall not drink
of the fruit of the vine
until the coming
of the kingdom of God."

The pericope, Luke 22, 15–18, is proper to the third Gospel. Neither Matthew nor Mark lingers over the description of the last Passover meal of Jesus with his disciples.

In the time of Jesus, the ritual celebration of the Passover meal comprised principally the eating of the Passover lamb and the blessing of three cups. The first part of the Hallel (Ps. 113–114) was sung after the second cup, and the second part of the Hallel (Ps. 115–118) after the third cup, which was called "the cup of blessing". These rites

which commemorated the past were also charged with the messianic
hopes proclaimed by the psalmists:

> Blessed be he who comes
> in the name of the Lord! (Ps. 118, 26).

This is the context in which Luke relates the eating of the Passover
(v. 15), the sharing of the cups (v. 17) and the hope of the "new earth
and new heaven" (vv. 18/16/18), where Jesus will celebrate the eternal
Passover with his own.

This context also forms a preface for the institution of the Supper,
itself the memorial of the Passover of Jesus (which Luke calls his
"exodus", 9, 31), and the herald of eternity.

Note also the hymn-like structure of the narrative whose two
"stanzas" (vv. 15-16 and 17-18) correspond and are strongly parallel
to one another, and form a diptych with the narrative of the institution
(vv. 19-20).

# The Institution of the Supper according to the Synoptic Gospels and the First Epistle to the Corinthians

# The Institution of the Supper according Epistle to the

The Institution of the Supper according to the Gospel the Co

| Matthew 26, 26–28 | Mark 14, 22–24 |
|---|---|
| 26. Now as they were eating, Jesus took bread, and blessed, and broke it, and gave it to the disciples, and said, "Take, eat. This is my body." | 22. And as they were eating, he took bread, and blessed, and broke it, and gave it to them, and said, "Take. This is my body." |
| 27. And he took a cup, and when he had given thanks he gave it to them, saying, "Drink of it, all of you, | 23. And he took a cup, and when he had given thanks he gave it to them, and they all drank of it. |
| 28. for this is my blood of the Covenant, which is poured out for many for the forgiveness of sins. | 24. And he said to them, "This is my blood of the Covenant, which is poured out for many. |
| 29. I tell you I shall not drink again of this fruit of the vine until that day when I drink it new with you in my Father's kingdom." | 25. Truly, I tell you I shall not drink again of the fruit of the vine until that day when I drink it new in the kingdom of God." |

# *to the Synoptic Gospels and the First Corinthians*

| Luke, 22, 19–20 | 1 Corinthians, 23b–25 |
|---|---|
| | 23b. The Lord Jesus<br>on the night he was betrayed<br>took bread, |
| 19. And he took bread, | |
| and when he had given thanks<br>he broke it,<br>and gave it to them,<br>saying,<br>"This is my body<br>which is given for you.<br>Do this<br>in memory of me". | 24. and when he had given thanks<br>he broke it,<br><br>and said,<br>"This is my body<br>which is (given) for you.<br>Do this<br>in memory of me". |
| 20. Likewise the cup,<br>after supper, | 25. In the same way also the cup,<br>after supper, |
| saying,<br>"This cup is<br>the new Covenant in my blood,<br>poured out for you. | saying,<br>"This cup is<br>the new Covenant in my blood.<br><br>Do this,<br>as often as you drink it,<br>in memory of me." |
| 18. For I tell you:<br>from now on I shall not drink<br>of the fruit of the vine<br><br>until the coming<br>of the kingdom of God." | 26. For as often<br>as you eat this bread<br>and drink the cup,<br>you proclaim<br>the Lord's death<br>until he comes. |

## *The narrative of the Institution*

The text of the Institution of the Supper[1] is attested by the synoptic writers Mark, Matthew and Luke, and by Paul, in the First Epistle to the Corinthians. If these four versions are compared with one another, there is a noticeable agreement between Matthew and Mark on the one hand, and between Luke and Paul on the other. This means that the primitive community knew the narrative in two versions, one represented by Matthew and Mark, the other by Luke and Paul.

Paul himself, as is well-known, refers to a "tradition"; "As for me, I received from the Lord that which in my turn I have handed on to you" (1 Cor. 11, 23a). Paul was living in Corinth from the end of the year 50 to the middle of the year 52 (Acts 18, 1-18). The text relating to the Eucharist dates therefore from the very first years of Christianity.

This was the text which was used by the primitive community in its celebrations and would be taken up in all the anaphoras: it was to form the nucleus of the eucharistic celebration of all subsequent Christians.

## *As they were eating, Jesus . . .*

Note the liturgical character of the introductory formulas of Matthew and Mark: "As they were eating, Jesus took bread. . . ." In the narrative of the Passion, into which the text of the institution is inserted, the mention of the meal is quite unnecessary since it merely repeats Mt. 26, 21 and Mk. 14, 18. On the contrary, it is wholly in place in a liturgical celebration where it emphasises the bond which links the Eucharist to the Passover meal and to its whole theological context. Paul, for his part, uses a formula of even greater solemnity, "The Lord Jesus", which is found in professions of faith (Rom. 10, 9 and 1 Cor. 12, 3), and adds "the night that he was betrayed", a phrase which evokes the figure of the Servant of Yahweh,[2] delivered up according to the designs of divine providence (Is. 53, 6, 12).

---

[1] The following notes on the narrative of the institution are reproduced from L. Deiss, *Synopse*, Desclée de Brouwer, Paris, 1963. The best exegetical analysis is that of J. Jeremias, *Die Abendmahlsworte Jesu*, 3rd ed., Göttingen, 1960.

[2] On the Servant of Yahweh, see p. 14, n. 1.

### The new Covenant in my blood

The formula "This cup is the new covenant in my blood" alludes to Exodus 24, 8: "This is the blood of the covenant that Yahweh has made with you". According to Matthew and Mark the blood of Jesus is poured out for *many*, that is to say, for all. For the underlying semitic expression, which the Greek translates as *many*, can have an exclusive sense (many, not therefore all) or an inclusive one (many, meaning all). The same semitic usage is found in the *logion* in Mark 10, 45 and Matthew 20, 28: "the Son of Man has come to give his life as a ransom for many", i.e. for all.[1] Taken together, these formulas again suggest the identification of Jesus with Isaiah's Servant of Yahweh:

| Matthew | Isaiah |
|---|---|
| This is my blood | I have appointed you |
| of the *covenant*, | as *covenant* of my people. (42, 6.) |
| poured out for *many* | And he bore upon himself |
| for the forgiveness of *sins*. | the *sins* of *many*. (53, 12.) |

The new covenant (Jer. 31, 31-34) which God makes with the whole human race is sealed by Jesus, the Servant of Yahweh, in the blood of his sacrifice.

### Do this in memory of me

The Eucharist celebrated by the Christian community is the memorial of the passion and of the resurrection of the Lord, of the entirety of the mysteries which go to make up his "Passover", that is to say, of his passing from this world to the glory of the Father. The formula, "in memory of me", seems to echo a prayer which was recited after the blessing of the third cup: "Our God, God of our fathers . . .

---

[1] Other examples of this usage: "Many are called", i.e., all are called, "but few are chosen" (Mt. 22, 14). "If by the fault of one (i.e., Adam) many (i.e., all men) have died, how much more are the grace of God and the gift given through the obedience of one man, Jesus Christ, spread abroad in profusion upon many (i.e., upon all men)."

remember the Messiah, the son of David, thy Servant . . ." (Passa-haggada). The apostles then were to celebrate the Eucharist in order that God might remember Jesus Messiah, the son of David (Ps. 132, 1), that is to say, that God might establish the kingdom inaugurated by Jesus in the triumphant fullness of eschatological times. This meaning is well brought out by the eucharistic prayer of the *Didache:* "Remember, Lord, thy Church, to deliver her from all evil and to make her perfect in thy love. Gather her together from the four winds, this holy Church, into the kingdom which thou hast prepared for her."[1]

---

[1] *Didache*, 10, 5: see p. 15.

# 2

# The Eucharistic Prayer of the Didache

# The Eucharistic Prayer of the Didache[1]

This is the most ancient eucharistic prayer yet known to us. In essence, it is a song of praise and blessing, like those which are found in the Old Testament and the Jewish liturgy, in which the chosen people celebrated the wonders of the salvation which God had brought about for them. Seen in the religious perspective of the New Testament, its subject is the supreme act of thanksgiving, the celebration of the Eucharist.

As for the Eucharist, give thanks like this:

First, for the cup:

We give thee thanks, our Father,
for the holy vine of David[2] thy servant
that thou hast revealed to us through Jesus, thy Child.
    Glory to thee for ever!

Next, for the broken bread:

---

[1] The definitive edition of the *Didache* was produced certainly between the years 100 and 150. Certain passages could even go back as far as the years 50–70, and thus be contemporary with the formation of the Pauline corpus and the sayings-collections found in the Gospels. On the *Didache*, see *Les Pères Apostoliques* (Vivante Tradition, 1), Fleurus, Paris.

[2] The mysterious expression, "the holy vine of David", with its suggestion of the prophetic style, seems here to stand for the entirety of salvation-history, especially for the inauguration of the New Covenant through the destruction on the cross and the glory of the resurrection. In his sermon at Pisidian Antioch Paul uses much the same idea: "As for us, we bring you the Good News: the promise which God made to our fathers he has fulfilled in our days for us their children, having raised Jesus from the dead, as it is written in the second psalm: *Thou art my son, this day I have begotten thee* (Ps. 2, 7). That God has raised him from the dead and that he will never again return to corruption, this indeed is what he had said: *I will give you the holy things of David, the things which are true*" (Acts 13, 32–34).

13

We give thee thanks, our Father,
for the life and the knowledge
that thou has revealed to us through Jesus, thy Child.[1]
    Glory to thee for ever!

Just as this bread which we break,
once scattered over the hills,
has been gathered and made one,
so may thy Church too be assembled
from the ends of the earth into thy kingdom!
For glory and power are thine for ever.

No one is to eat or drink your Eucharist
except those who have been baptised in the name of the Lord;
for in this regard the Lord said:
"Do not give holy things to the dogs."[2]

After you have eaten your fill, give thanks like this:

We give thee thanks, O holy Father,
for thy holy name
which thou hast made to dwell in our hearts,

---

[1] The application of the word *child* to Jesus is characteristic of the oldest Christian texts. The Greek word *pais* which it translates oscillates between the two meanings *child* and *servant*. The primitive community, meditating on the Servant poems of Isaiah (42, 1–9; 49, 1–6; 50, 4–11; and especially 52, 13–53, 12), had seen in them a prophecy of the vocation of Jesus, *the holy Servant* (Acts 4, 27, 30, cf. 3, 26; Mt. 8, 17 = Is. 53, 4; Mt. 12, 18–21 = Is. 42, 1–4; Lk. 22, 37 = Is. 53, 12). The application of these texts to Jesus was made even easier by the fact that the Hebrew word *ebed*, servant, too, could mean *child* or *son*. It was therefore extremely useful for expressing the mystery of Jesus, *Servant* of God in his messianic and redemptive vocation, but beloved *Son* of the Father by origin, the Servant humbled in the sufferings of the passion, but *"constituted Son of God with power . . . through his resurrection from the dead"* (Rom. 1, 4). In addition, the figure of the Servant of Yahweh in Isaiah has both an individual and a collective character, and this suggested the ecclesial dimension of the vocation of Jesus, involving as he does the whole community of the faithful in his passion and his resurrection. When, therefore, the oldest Christian texts apply the word *child* to Jesus, it is charged with all this weight of history and theology.

[2] Mt. 7, 6.

for the knowledge, faith and immortality
that thou hast revealed to us through Jesus, thy Child.
  Glory to thee for ever!


It is thou, almighty Master, who hast created the world,
that thy name may be praised;
for their enjoyment thou hast given
food and drink to the children of men;
but us thou hast graciously favoured
with a spiritual food
and with a drink that gives eternal life,
  through Jesus, thy Child.


Above all, we give thee thanks
for thine own great power.
  Glory to thee for ever!
  Amen.


Remember, Lord, thy Church,
to deliver her from all evil,
to make her perfect in thy love.
Gather her from the four winds,
this Church thou hast sanctified,[1]
into the kingdom thou hast prepared for her.
For power and glory are thine for ever.
  Amen.

---

[1] Throughout this prayer the word *Church* preserves its Old Testament significance, meaning *the assembly of the children of Israel gathered by the Word of God for the celebration of the Covenant* (see Deut. 23, 2-4, 9). In the same way, under the New Covenant, the Lord gathers his Church from the four winds by calling all the faithful into the eternal kingdom of Jesus.

May the Lord come[1] and may this world pass away!
    Amen.
Hosanna to the house of David!
He who is holy, let him approach.
He who is not, let him do penance.
    Marana tha![2]
    Amen.

*Didache* 9 *and* 10

---

[1] "May the Lord come" (cf. Apoc. 22, 20): this is according to the Coptic
ersion; another variant is: "Let grace come".
[2] An Aramaic expression which had become a liturgical term and which
means: *Lord, come!* (I Cor. 16, 22; cf. Apoc. 22, 20; Rom. 13, 12; Phil. 4, 5; James 5,
8; I Pet. 4, 7). It can also be read as *Maran atha*, meaning: *the Lord comes*.

# 3

# The Witness of Saint Justin
## *(about 150 A.D.)*

# Saint Justin

## The man

Justin was born in the heart of Galilee, at Flavia Neapolis, a pagan Roman town, built on the site of the ancient Shechem, not far from the well of Jacob. Although he came from so close to the well where Jesus had promised the Samaritan woman the living water which would quench her thirst for ever and spring up to life everlasting, Justin was yet ignorant of Christ. Thirsting for God, he set out across the world in search of the truth.

He put himself first in the hands of a Stoic. It was his first disappointment, for this self-styled master "knew nothing of God and did not even think the knowledge necessary".

He tried his luck next with a Peripatetic. But this disciple of Aristotle did not have the same greatness of soul as his master and expected to be paid for teaching the truth. So when he began by demanding his fees, Justin was disheartened and himself brought the lesson to an end.

In the same way he trusted himself to a Pythagorean, but this man wanted to do the preliminary studies in music, astronomy and geometry. Justin was in a hurry, feverishly impatient to get to essentials.

In the midst of all this a Platonist came on the scene, to whom Justin attached himself believing that he had a real grasp of the truth.

He was disillusioned again but for the last time, for now he encountered Christ, was dazzled and spell-bound:

> A fire blazed up suddenly in my soul. I was seized with love for the prophets and for these men who had loved Christ; I reflected on all these words and decided that this philosophy alone was true and profitable.
>
> That is how I became and why I am a philosopher. And I wish that all men felt the same way as I do.[1]

---

[1] *Dialogue with Trypho*, 8. *P.G.* 6, 492 CD.

At the same time as he encountered Christ, Justin also came in contact with Christians; the life of the disciples seemed to him to be worthy of their Master and their superb disdain of death reduced to nothing the accusations which ill-wishers peddled against them:

> I myself, in the days when the teachings of Plato were my delight, used to listen to the accusations made against Christians. But when I saw how fearless they were in the face of death, of terrors of every kind, I realised that it was impossible that they should be leading vicious and pleasure-seeking lives. Why indeed should a man who loved pleasure and debauchery, who liked eating human flesh, go looking for death, which would deprive him of all these pleasures? Surely he would try at all costs to preserve this present life, to keep out of the way of the magistrates, rather than denounce himself to them and so get himself sentenced to death?[1]

After his conversion, which took place almost certainly at Ephesus about the year 130, he set off on his travels again as a wandering philosopher. He came to Rome during the reign of Antoninus Pius (138–161), founded a Christian school there and was martyred somewhere between 156 and 166.

Before he died he wrote the following words, most moving in themselves and forming a very beautiful conclusion to his work:

> Nobody believed in Socrates deeply enough to die for his teaching. . . . But for Christ, not only philosophers and men of letters, but even artisans and uneducated men have made light of fame, fear and death.[2]

His feast is celebrated liturgically on 14 April.

---

[1] *Second Apology*, 12; P.G. 6, 464 AB.
[2] *Ibid.*, 10; P.G. 6, 461 AB.

# His work

Of the considerable body of work which Justin produced, there still survive the two *Apologies* and the *Dialogue with the Jew Trypho*.

The two *Apologies* were written in Rome about the year 150 (at one point Justin tells us that Christ was born 150 years before). The dedication of the work is of a splendid loftiness and audacity: "To the emperor Antoninus Pius . . . and to his son Verissimus (Marcus Aurelius) . . . to the sacred Senate and to the whole Roman people, I address this discourse and petition for men of every race who are unjustly hated and persecuted, I who am one of them, Justin, son of Priscus, son of Baccheius, a native of Flavia Neapolis in Palestine." *I, one of them*—the words are mad in their openness. Justin knows that Christians are being martyred, that merely to bear the name of Christian is considered a crime. It does not matter. He will not take the trouble to disguise his authorship. He cries out his faith.

It is in this proclamation of his faith that we find the passages which are our particular concern, those which describe Christian initiation, the celebration of the Eucharist and of the Lord's Day. These passages are eighteen hundred years old, but in them the liturgy of the second century comes to life again.

## Christian initiation

We are going to outline for you how we are renewed by Christ and consecrate ourselves to God. To omit this would seem to be a fault in our exposition.

Those who believe in the truth of our teaching and our words promise first of all to live according to this doctrine. Then we teach them to pray and to beg pardon of God, with fasting, for their past sins. And we too pray and fast with them.[1]

Then we lead them to a place where there is water and they

---

[1] The preparation of converts for baptism involves on the one hand teaching on the Christian faith (*Apol. I*, 61) and on moral living (I, 61 and 66) and on the other the practice of prayer and fasting. Fasting before baptism is already attested by the interpolated text of the *Didache*, 7, 4; see J.-P. Audet, *La Didaché, Instruction des apôtres*, Paris, 1958, p. 233.

are re-born in the same way that we were re-born ourselves. They are purified, that is, in the water, in the name of God the Father and Master of the Universe, of Jesus Christ, our Saviour, and of the Holy Spirit. Christ indeed said: "If you are not born again, you shall not enter into the kingdom of heaven."[1] That it is impossible for those who have once been born to enter again into their mother's womb, is evident to everyone. This is why the prophet Isaiah, whom I mentioned earlier, teaches us the way in which sinners must turn from their sins and repent. He puts it like this:

> Wash yourselves, purify yourselves,
> remove the evil from your soul,
> learn to do good.
> Be just to the orphan
> and defend the widow.
> Then come and let us talk together, says the Lord:
> Though your sins were like purple,
> they shall become white like wool;
> and if they are like scarlet,
> they shall become white like snow.
> But if you do not obey,
> the sword shall devour you.
> The mouth of the Lord has spoken this.[2]

Such is the teaching that the Apostles have handed down to us on this matter (. . .).

On him who wishes to be re-born and repents of his sins, we invoke the name of God, Father and Master of the universe (. . .).

This washing is called "enlightenment" because those who are taught in this way are enlightened in spirit.

---

[1] A free quotation from John 3, 5.
[2] A free quotation from Isaiah 1, 16–20.

(We invoke too) on him who is enlightened and purified the name of Jesus Christ, who was crucified under Pontius Pilate, and of the Holy Spirit, who foretold the whole story of Jesus through the prophets.

*Apol. I,* 61.

## The celebration of the Eucharist

### The *communal prayers*

As for us, after the one who believes and has given his assent has been purified, we lead him to the place where those who are called the "brethren" are assembled.

We pray fervently together for ourselves, for him who has just been enlightened, and for all the rest in whatever place they may be, that, having come to know the truth, we may be judged worthy to practise good works, keep the commandments and so obtain everlasting salvation.

### The *kiss of peace*

When the prayers are finished, we give each other the kiss (of peace).

### *Anaphora*

Then bread and a cup of wine to which water has been added are brought to the one who is presiding over the assembly of the brethren.

He takes them, gives praise and glory to the Father of the universe, through the name of the Son and of the Holy Spirit,

and then makes a long eucharist,[1] for having been judged worthy
of these good things.

When he has finished, all the people present acclaim it
saying: "Amen".[2] Amen is a Hebrew word which means: so be it.

*Apol. I,* 65.

## Communion

When the president has finished the eucharist and all the
people have acclaimed it, those whom we call deacons distribute
the consecrated bread, and water and wine, to each of those who
are present and take some away to those who are not.

*Apol. I,* 65.

We call this food "Eucharist". No one can have a share in
it unless he has undergone the washing which forgives sins and
regenerates, and unless he lives according to the teaching of
Christ. For we do not take this food as though it were ordinary
bread and wine. But, just as through the Word of God Jesus
Christ became incarnate, took flesh and blood for our salvation,
in the same way this food, which has become Eucharist thanks to
the prayer formed out of the words of Christ, and which nourishes
and is assimilated into our flesh and blood, is the flesh and blood
of incarnate Jesus: this is the doctrine that we have received.

For indeed the Apostles, in those memoirs of theirs which are
called "Gospels", tell us that Jesus gave them this command:
having taken bread, he gave thanks and said: "Do this in memory
of me, this is my body"; in the same way, having taken the cup,
he gave thanks and said: "This is my blood." And it was to them
alone that he gave them.

*Apol. I,* 65–66.

---

[1] That is, a thanksgiving.

[2] Although one of the simple faithful, Justin has a lofty idea of his own
participation in the eucharistic prayer, a participation expressed by his Amen which
concludes the prayer of the presiding priest.

## The Liturgy of the Lord's day

### A community of charity and prayer

Those who are well-to-do come to the help of those who are in need, and we always lend one another assistance.

In all that we offer, we bless the Creator of the universe through his Son Jesus Christ and through the Holy Spirit.

### The celebration of the Lord's day

On the day which is called Sun-day, all, whether they live in the town or in the country, gather in the same place.

Then the Memoirs of the Apostles or the Writings of the Prophets are read for as long as time allows.[1]

When the reader has finished, the president speaks, exhorting us to live by these noble teachings.

Then we rise all together[2] and pray.

---

[1] The Mass as described by Justin already shows the essential elements of the Christian celebration—the reading of the Word of God, the president's homily, prayer in common, Eucharist. It is interesting to note that "the fundamental connection between the Eucharist and the proclamation of the Word of God seems to have been perceived from the first by the Christian community" (J. Lécuyer, *Le Sacrifice de la Nouvelle Alliance*, 1961, p. 229). The community of Justin, like the community of the Book of Acts, is built up "in the teaching of the apostles and the breaking of bread" (Acts 2, 42).

[2] In the ancient church, the regular attitude of prayer was to stand upright. This was more than an attitude of respect towards God, more too than a simple survival of Jewish tradition; it was above all the expression of the holy enfranchisement which the Lord had brought his faithful through his resurrection; it was too the sign of the expectation of the Lord, an expectation especially alive on Sunday, since that day was a kind of anticipation of the eternal Day of God: "We stand up when we pray, on the first day of the week (i.e., Sunday). . . . This is not only because, risen with Christ and having to seek the things above (Col. 3, 1), we call to mind the grace given us, by standing upright when we pray on that day consecrated to the resurrection, but also because that day itself seems in some fashion to be an image of the world to come" (St Basil, *On the Holy Spirit*, 27; see B. Pruche, *Basile de Césarée, Traité du Saint Esprit*, Sources chrétiennes, 17, Paris 1945, pp. 236–237).

Then, as we said earlier, when the prayer is finished, bread, wine and water are brought. The president then prays and gives thanks as well as he can.[1] And all the people reply with the acclamation: Amen!

After this the eucharists are distributed and shared out to everyone, and the deacons are sent to take them to those who are absent.

Those who are well-to-do and desire to, make gifts each just as he wishes. These gifts are collected and handed over to the president. He it is who assists the orphans and widows, those who are in want through sickness or for some other reason, prisoners, strangers passing through; briefly, who helps all who are in need.

We hold this meeting of us all on Sun-day because it is the first day, the day when God transformed matter and darkness and created the world, and also because it was on this same day that Jesus Christ, our Saviour, rose from the dead. He was crucified on the eve of Saturn's day,[2] and on the morrow of this day, that is to say Sun-day, he appeared to his apostles and disciples and taught them this doctrine that we have submitted to your scrutiny.

*Apol. I,* 67.

---

[1] In the prayer of the anaphora, the president improvises freely on a basic outline. See note, p. 49, n. 2.

[2] That is, Friday, the eve of Saturn's day, our present Saturday.

# 4

# The Apostolic Tradition of Hippolytus of Rome

## (about 215 A.D.)

# Hippolytus of Rome

## The man

In 212 A.D., the young Origen undertook a journey to Rome to get to know, as he himself put it, "the very ancient church of the Romans". He had occasion to hear a sermon on *the praise of our Lord and Saviour*. The preacher was called Hippolytus. He was a simple priest of the Roman church. But the prestige of his immense learning, his real talent for writing and his numerous personal relationships had placed him in the forefront of the religious life of the age. His profound knowledge of Greek philosophy and his astonishing familiarity with the eastern mystery-cults lead one to believe that he was not of Roman or Latin origin, but came from the East.

At this time the trinitarian conflicts had turned Rome into a theological battlefield. These doctrines were hotly debated and caused many a fierce quarrel. The "monarchians" insisted strongly on the unity of the Trinity but ran the risk of underemphasising the Trinity of persons; the anti-monarchians stressed the distinction of persons but on their part risked casting doubt on the godhead of the Word. Hippolytus who, if we are to believe Photius, gave himself out to be a disciple of Irenaeus, meaning by that that he shared his master's zeal for the defence of the traditional doctrine, threw himself into the struggle with all the weight of his knowledge and of his fiery temperament. But, as often happens in such cases, an excess of zeal for the true faith can lead a man into an extreme position.[1] Hippolytus thought that the blame was to be thrown on Pope Zephyrinus (198–217) whom he accused of secretly favouring the monarchian heresy. In fact the Pope, who was little versed in theological subtleties or interested in

---

[1] See A. D'Alès, *La Théologie de saint Hippolyte*, Paris, 1906. Hippolytus' doctrinal position on the Word is especially vulnerable to criticism and could lead normally to affirming the existence of two gods. It is quite understandable that Callistus should describe Hippolytus and his followers as "worshippers of two gods", despite the anger of the latter in the face of such an accusation (*Philosophoumena*, 9.12, 4; *P.G.* 16, 3383 C).

anguishing metaphysics, had hardly any intention of intervening in the actual debate. He was a pleasant man with the wisdom of old age, which on this occasion was to re-state the formulas bequeathed him by tradition, although he risked drawing down on himself the reputation of ignorance. The ambiguity of certain declarations gave Hippolytus a considerable advantage against him.[1]

The situation was strained enough, when the Pope died. In 218 the clergy of Rome chose Callistus to succeed him.

Callistus was a former slave whose past had been somewhat disturbed, but who was also a confessor of the faith who had had the good luck to return alive from prison. He had been the principal deacon of Zephyrinus, charged with the temporal administration of the Church. His accession to the pontificate could therefore only render Hippolytus disaffected. He transferred his former opposition to Zephyrinus to the new Pope.

The situation became further inflamed when Callistus decided to mitigate the discipline of the Church relating to those who had sinned gravely. Hippolytus thought such indulgence was weakness. He chose in the end a solution of despair, left the Church, had himself elected bishop of Rome by an influential group of clergy, founded a new church in opposition to the Roman community and so became the first anti-pope.

He persevered in his schism even when Callistus was replaced by Urban (223–230) and Urban in his turn by Pontian (230–235).

---

[1] In the *Philosophoumena*, 9, 12 (*P.G.* 16, 3386 AC), he wrote: "The first (Callistus) dared to legitimise acts of pleasure, saying that he could forgive sins for all the world. Anyone who had been led astray by another, so long as he was Christian in name, could receive pardon if he joined the school of Callistus. . . . In these cases he used to apply the words of the Apostle: 'Who art thou to judge the servant of another?' (Rom. 14, 4). He even held that the parable of the tares, 'Let the tares go on growing with the wheat' (Mt. 13, 30), had been taught us for this very reason, that is, for those who commit sins after their entry into the Church. He said also that the ark of Noah was a type of the Church, that ark which held dogs, wolves, ravens and all animals, whether pure or impure: so too, he claimed, it must be in the Church." These accusations, even when one allows for a certain amount of rhetorical untrustworthiness and personal polemic, demonstrate the high idea which Hippolytus had of the holiness of the Church. They did not, however, lead to the condemnation of Callistus by history. The Pope, in fact, could have had very good reasons of a pastoral order for softening penitential discipline. Besides, he is remembered in the Church without any stigma and history has never had to disavow him. For further information consult A. D'Alès, *L'Édit de Calliste*, Paris, 1914, especially ch. 7, "Le Témoignage de saint Hippolyte", pp. 217–227.

There seemed to be no way out of this unhappy situation, when religious persecution provided an unexpected solution, a solution which allowed both parties to triumph, but on a different level. The moment he achieved power, Maximinus the Thracian (235–238) issued an edict which outlawed the heads of the churches; their crime was that they had preached the Gospel. Pontian and Hippolytus, pope and anti-pope, both found themselves in extermination camps, which in those days were the mines of Sardinia. Communion in suffering opened the way to communion in faith and charity. Pontian resigned on 28 September, 235. Hippolytus did the same, so entering once more into the unity of the Church. Both died martyrs on "the island of death".

Pope Fabian (236–250) had their bodies brought back to Rome. Their funerals took place on the same day, 13 August, 236 or 237. So it comes about that on 13 August every year the Church celebrates the memory of St Hippolytus, anti-pope and martyr "whose witness to the truth serves our salvation".[1]

## The work

The list of Hippolytus' writings is considerable. Unfortunately, many of his works seem to be irrecoverably lost, buried under the rubbish of eighteen centuries, rotted or burnt in the ruins of ancient libraries. To time's neglect was added man's. For Hippolytus wrote in Greek, and, after his death, the knowledge of the Greek language became less and less usual in Rome. And Roman tradition, remembering that Hippolytus had been an anti-pope, would not trouble itself unduly over the loss of works whose orthodoxy was somewhat suspect and which were written in a language it no longer used.

Among the writings which have survived the wreck are to be found works of controversy such as the *Philosophoumena* or *Refutation of All Heresies* (after 222), which is somewhat reminiscent of Irenaeus'

---

[1] Secret of the Mass, 13 August. On Callistus and his age, the following may be consulted: Fliche/Martin, *Histoire de l'Église*, Vol. 2, Paris, 1948, pp. 101–106 and 404–407; E. Amann, art. on Hippolytus, *D.T.C.*, vol. 6, col. 2487–2493. More complete bibliographies are to be found in the manuals of patrology. F. Cayré, *Patrologie et Histoire de la Théologie*, Vol. 1, Paris, 1953, p. 239; J. Quasten, *Initiation aux Pères de l'Église*, Vol. 2, Paris, 1957, pp. 195 ff; Altaner-Chirat, *Précis de Patrologie* Mulhouse, 1961, pp. 250 ff.

*Against Heresies*, and the *Demonstration against the Jews*; dogmatic writings like the treatise *On Antichrist* (about 202); exegetical works such as the commentaries *On Daniel*, *On the Song of Songs*, *The History of David and Goliath*, and *On the Psalms*, commentaries in which he adopts, but tones down, the allegorical and typological method of interpretation so dear to Origen. We possess also some chronological treatises such as *The Determination of the Date of Easter* (222) and above all the *Chronicle*, a work in which he exerts himself to calm the impatience of certain Christians who thought that the end of the world was imminent (he reckoned that the world was 5738 years old and was to last at least until the year 6000).

Various homilies also are worth mentioning, for example *On Easter*, *On the Heresy of Noetus*, *On the Praise of the Lord our Saviour*. And lastly we must take note of the work which is of special interest here, the *Apostolic Tradition*.

Several of these works have come down to us in different translations, Latin, Syriac, Coptic, Arabic, Ethiopian, Armenian, Georgian and Slavonic, the variety of which shows the interest which eastern Christianity took in this Roman theologian. Again, the mass and variety of the writings themselves bear witness how hard Hippolytus laboured in the cause of the Christian faith. And just as men usually attribute things only to the rich, so several works were attributed to him which in fact he did not write.

## The Apostolic Tradition

No other writing of Hippolytus has roused so much interest among theologians, especially among liturgists, as the discovery and identification of the *Apostolic Tradition*. This work, whose production goes back to 215, represents far the richest source that we possess today for the understanding of the constitution of the Roman church and her liturgy at the beginning of the third century. Its discovery was a real triumph for scientific research.

In 1551 a statue of Hippolytus was dug up in a Roman cemetery on the Via Tiburtina, the Agro Verano. On its pediment was engraved a list of his works, and there, among others, the following title was to be read:

(AP)OSTOLIKE PARADOSIS

that is "Apostolic Tradition". The question was what had become of this work.

A work known as the *Canons of Hippolytus*, an Arabic translation from a Coptic one, had been known since 1870. But this work as a whole was mistrusted by the scholars since it appeared to be a compilation from different sources and it did not seem possible to identify it with the *Apostolic Tradition*. Nevertheless an undeniable relationship could be shown to exist between the *Canons of Hippolytus* and certain other documents, such as the *Apostolic Constitutions*, a Greek compilation of Syrian origin dating from the end of the fourth century,[1] the *Testament of our Lord*, of Syrian origin and dating probably from the fifth century, and above all *The Egyptian Church Order*. These were the sites on which it was necessary to excavate in order to find the *Apostolic Tradition*. The tentative exploring took a long time. First there was E. Schwartz,[2] who suspected that the missing work survived in the *Egyptian Church Order* and published his hypothesis in 1910. Six years later, in 1916, without knowing the work of his predecessor, R. H. Connolly[3] succeeded in proving firmly that the *Egyptian Church Order* was the basis of all the other compilations and was effectively to be identified with the *Apostolic Tradition* of Hippolytus.

On its journey down to us the primitive text had had a lively history. Hippolytus had indeed written it in Greek. The original was lost, but a Latin translation had been made, without doubt at the beginning of the fourth century; this was discovered on a palimpsest in the Chapter Library at Verona. It is fragmentary—a good many leaves are missing—but very faithful, so much so that the Greek original can often be seen behind the mistakes and misinterpretations of the translator. In order to fill in the gaps in the Latin, recourse must be had to the oriental texts. The *Egyptian Church Order* represents translations into Coptic—first into Sahidic and then into Bohairic[4]—into Arabic and into Ethiopian. These are not all of equal value.

---

[1] See pp. 151–183.

[2] Ed. Schwartz, *Ueber die pseudoapostolischen Kirchenordnungen*, in *Schriften der Wissensch. Gesellsch. in Strassburg*, 6, Strasburg, 1910.

[3] R. H. Connolly, *The So-Called Egyptian Church Order and Derived Documents*, in *Texts and Studies* VIII, 4, Cambridge, 1916.

[4] Sahidic (saidi) is the dialect of Upper Egypt, Bohairic (beheri) of Lower Egypt.

The Sahidic seems to be the closest to the original. The Arabic
translation, and without doubt the Ethiopian, depend on the Sahidic.
By comparing these different sources we can conjecturally reconstitute the text and translate it back into the original Greek.

# First Part

## The Liturgy of Holy Orders

### 2-3. *The Bishop*

Let him be ordained bishop who has been chosen by all the
people.[1] When he has been appointed and approved by all, let
the people come together with the college of priests and bishops
who are present, on the Lord's Day.[2] On the consent of all, let
these latter lay their hands on him. The priests attend in silence.
Let all be quiet and pray in their hearts that the Holy Spirit may
come down.

Let one of the bishops present, at the demand of all, lay
his hands on him who is to receive episcopal ordination and pray
in these terms.[3]

God and Father of our Lord Jesus Christ,

---

[1] Hippolytus insists on the participation of the entire community in the
designation of the future bishop: he is elected by all, approved by all and receives
the laying on of hands by the consent and at the demand of all.

[2] Sunday.

[3] What follows is the "prayer of consecration"; it accompanies and makes
explicit the rite of the laying on of hands by which the episcopate is conferred.
These splendid formulas develop the theme of the episcopal ministry so fully that
they were often to be re-introduced as "prayers for the Bishop" or even "prayers
for the Pope".

Father of mercy and all consolation,[1]
thou who dwellest in the highest of the heavens
and dost lower thy regard to him who is humble,[2]
who knowest all things before they exist;
who hast fixed the bounds of thy Church
by the word of thy grace;
who hast predestined from the beginning
the race of the just of Abraham;
who hast established leaders and priests,
who hast not left thy sanctuary without worship;
who hast set thy pleasure, since the foundation of the world,
in being glorified by those whom thou hast chosen:

Pour out now the power
which has its origin in thee,
the sovereign Spirit[3] whom thou hast given
to thy beloved Child Jesus Christ[4]
and that he has handed on to the apostles
who built the Church in place of thy sanctuary[5]
for the glory and unceasing praise of thy name.

Grant, O Father who readest the heart,
that thy servant whom thou has chosen as bishop
may feed thy holy flock,
may exercise thy sovereign priesthood without reproach
serving thee day and night.

---

[1] 2 Cor. 1, 3.

[2] An allusion to Ps. 113, 5-6: "He is enthroned in the heights and descends to see the heavens and the earth".

[3] A formula borrowed from Ps. 51, 14 in the Septuagint version.

[4] An archaising formula (see p. 14, n. 1) of the Greek text. The Latin has: "to thy beloved Son Jesus Christ".

[5] The former temple which was replaced by the Church of the new Covenant.

May he never cease to render thy regard favourable,
and offer to thee the gifts of thy holy Church.
In virtue of the Spirit of the supreme priesthood,
may he have the power to forgive sins
according to thy commandment.

May he distribute the shares following thine order;
may he loose every bond in virtue of the power
that thou hast conferred on the apostles.[1]
May he be pleasing to thee
for gentleness and purity of heart.
May he be before thee a sweet savour
through thy Child Jesus Christ, our Lord.

Through him, glory to thee, power and honour,
Father and Son, with the Holy Spirit,
in thy holy Church,[2]
now and always
and for ever and ever!
    Amen.

## 4. *The Anaphora*

Immediately after his consecration and the kiss of peace the newly ordained bishop celebrates the Eucharist. He does so in union "with the whole college of priests"; it is therefore a real concelebration.

By great good fortune we possess the anaphora[3] of this first

---

[1] The text alludes to Mt. 18, 18 and Jn. 20, 22–23.

[2] "In thy Church" is found only in the Ethiopian version. The words belong to the formula of the doxology traditional in Hippolytus; see p. 43, n. 1.

[3] In classical Greek *anaphora* means the offering (literally the elevation) of a sacrifice to a god. In liturgical language, the word refers to the prayer of offering in the eucharistic liturgy, a prayer of which the essential elements are the recitation of the institution of the Supper and the words of consecration. In the liturgy of the Roman mass, the anaphora corresponds to the canon, with the preface by which it is introduced. On the text of Hippolytus, see P. Cagin, *L'Anaphore apostolique*, Paris, 1919.

episcopal mass. Through the formulas which Hippolytus has handed down to us we can see how the mass was celebrated in Rome in 215. This anaphora of course does not represent the only type that existed in the Roman liturgy at that time, but it is the only one that has come down to us from that ancient period; it is too the earliest in all Christian literature.

Neither does Hippolytus intend to impose a text. He only proposes it,[1] safeguarding the right of the celebrant to improvise freely himself, safeguarding also the right of the Spirit to inspire other formulas of prayer in the heart and on the lips of the celebrant, who represents Christ in the eyes of the community.

It is worth drawing attention to the clear Christological character of this anaphora; also, to the absence of the Sanctus, which was soon to become traditional, and of any mention of the wonders of creation and salvation-history, the *mirabilia Dei*. Hippolytus' extreme conciseness brings out magnificently the movement of the eucharistic prayer. The anaphora is resplendent in its primitive simplicity. It is not yet burdened with any of those flourishes with which later centuries were pleased to ornament it and which, like a luxuriant but parasitic growth, often ran the risk of hiding the beauty which they were intended to enhance.

Although it was forgotten in Rome for centuries, this ancient anaphora of Hippolytus is still recited today by Abyssinian priests. The voice of the Roman martyr still resounds on the soil of Africa.

## Acclamation

When he has been consecrated bishop, let all give him the kiss of peace and acclaim him with the words: "He has become worthy".[2]

---

[1] *Apostolic Tradition*, 10; see p. 49. This freedom is equally underlined b Justin who writes: "The president then prays and gives thanks *as well as he can*" (*Apology* I, 67; see p. 26).

[2] Another possible translation is: "And salute him because he has become worthy" (B. Botte, *La Tradition apostolique*, Sources chrétiennes, 11, Paris, 1946, p. 30).

Let the deacons present the offering to him. When he lays
his hands on it, with the whole college of priests, let him say
the words of thanksgiving:

— The Lord be with you.
— And with thy spirit.
— Let us lift up our hearts.
— They are turned to the Lord.
— Let us give thanks to the Lord.
— It is worthy and just.


*Thanksgiving*

Let him continue thus:

We give thee thanks, O God,
through thy beloved Child,[1] Jesus Christ,
whom thou hast sent to us in the last times[2]
as Saviour, Redeemer and Messenger of thy will.
He is thine inseparable Word
through whom thou hast created all things
and in whom thou art well pleased.


Thou didst send him from heaven
into the womb of a Virgin.
He was conceived and became incarnate,
he manifested himself as thy Son,
born of the Spirit and the Virgin.[3]

---

[1] See p. 14, n. 1.

[2] I.e., messianic times, considered as the "last times" of the history of salvation;
see Acts 2, 17.

[3] A similar formula is found again in Hippolytus, in his sermon *On the heresy
of Noetus*, 4 (P.G. 10, 810 B): "The flesh offered by the Word of the Father . . .
(coming) from the Spirit and the Virgin, manifested as perfect Son of God."

He accomplished thy will
and, to acquire a holy people for thee,
he stretched out his hands while he suffered
to deliver from suffering
those who believe in thee.


*Account of the Institution*

When he gave himself up willingly to suffering
to destroy death,
to break the fetters of the devil,
to trample hell under his feet,
to spread his light abroad over the just,
to establish the Covenant
and manifest his Resurrection,[1]
he took bread,
he gave thee thanks and said:
"Take, eat, this is my body
which is broken for you."
Likewise for the chalice, he said:
This is my blood
which is poured out for you.
When you do this,
do (it) in memory of me.

---

[1] These formulas seem to have undergone the influence of Irenaeus, who wrote in the *Demonstration of the Apostolic Preaching*, 38: "God the Father then was full of mercy; he sent the Word . . . (who) undid the chains of (our) prison. And his light appeared and dissipated the darkness of the prison and sanctified our birth and destroyed death, undoing those very bonds in which we had been chained. And he showed his resurrection, becoming himself the first-born from the dead." See L. M. Froidevaux, *Irénée de Lyon, Démonstration de la prédication apostolique* (Sources chrétiennes), Paris, 1959, p. 92.

*Anamnesis*[1]

We then, remembering thy death
and thy Resurrection,
offer thee bread and wine,
we give thee thanks for having judged us worthy
to stand before thee and serve thee.


*Epiclesis*[2]

And we beg thee
to send thy Holy Spirit
upon the offering of thy holy Church,
to gather and unite
all those who receive it.
May they be filled with the Holy Spirit
who strengthens their faith in the truth.
So may we be able to praise and glorify thee
through thy Child Jesus Christ.

---

[1] The *anamnesis* (Greek, remembrance) is the prayer which commemorates the mysteries of salvation contained in the celebration of the eucharist. It is based on our Lord's words: "Do this *in memory* of me". The corresponding prayer in the Roman liturgy is the *Unde et memores*. See A. Croegaert, *Les rites et prières du saint sacrifice de la Messe*, vol. 3, Malines, 1948, pp. 184 ff and bibliography, p. 209.

[2] The *epiclesis* (Greek, invocation) is the prayer which invokes the descent of the Holy Spirit on the offerings (see A. Croegaert, loc. cit., pp. 223–228). It is to be found in all the Eastern liturgies and in many Western ones. It has disappeared from the Roman rite (see N. M. Denis-Boulet, *Analyse des rites et des prières de la messe*, in A. G. Martimort, *L'Église en prière*, Paris, 1961, pp. 405–408. On the theological significance of the Epiclesis, see M. De La Taille, *Mysterium Fidei*, Paris, 1924, pp. 446–452).

*Doxology*

> Through him, glory to thee, and honour,
> to the Father and to the Son, with the Holy Spirit,
> in thy holy Church,
> now and for ever.
> Amen.

## Blessing of the offerings of the faithful

Immediately after the anaphora, Hippolytus sets out some formulas of blessing for the offerings presented by the faithful.

The insertion of these blessings at this point in the eucharistic liturgy seems to correspond to a very precise theological plan,[1] to what today we would call the theology of earthly realities, and which is of great beauty.

In offering the Eucharist, Irenaeus[2] explains, the Church presents the first-fruits of the created world to God. She offers the body of Christ, but under the sign of the "bread which comes from the created world"; she offers his blood under the sign of "the cup which comes from this created world of ours". Thus the offerings presented by the faithful for the bishop's blessing are set within the radiance of the Eucharist; they are made holy in the prolongation of the thanks-

---

[1] Hippolytus in fact could well have situated these blessings in chapter 28 where he treats explicitly of offerings; see p. 66. The Roman liturgy in a similar way has preserved a blessing of the offerings of the faithful within the Canon (the doxology *Per quem omnia* which closes it). In this connection J. A. Jungmann notes that "from the origins of the Roman canon up to and beyond the end of the Middle Ages, a blessing of the fruits of the earth was, in various circumstances, carried out at this point" (*Missarum Solemnia*, Paris, 1954, vol. 3, p. 182).

[2] "To his disciples (Christ) gave counsel that they should offer the first-fruits of his creatures. Certainly God has no need of them: it is rather that they should not be found lacking in (spiritual) fruits and in gratitude. He took therefore bread which comes from the created world and gave thanks, saying: 'This is my body'. He did the same for the chalice which comes from this created world of ours. He announced that it was his blood, he taught that it was the Covenant of the New Testament. The Church received this offering from the apostles, she offers it throughout the whole world to God who gives us food, *as first-fruits of his gifts in the New Testament*" (*Adv. Haer.*, iv, 17, 5; *P.G.* 7, 1023 B–C).

giving which changes the offered bread and wine into the body and
blood of Christ.[1]

## 6. Blessing of oil

If a man offers oil, let him give thanks as for bread, not in
the same terms but in the same sense. Let him say:

O God, in making this oil holy
thou givest holiness
to those who use it and who receive it.
Through it thou didst confer anointing
on kings, priests and prophets.
Let it procure likewise
consolation for those who taste it
and health for those who make use of it.

## Blessing of cheese and olives

Likewise, if a man offers cheese and olives, let him pray thus:

Make this curdled milk holy
by uniting us to thy charity.[2]
Let this fruit of the olive
never lose its sweetness.
It is the symbol of the abundance
which thou hast made to flow from the tree (of the Cross)
for all those who hope in thee.

---

[1] J. A. Jungmann gives the same explanation: "If the insertion is made at this
point, it is because the Church wished to link her own acts of blessing to the great
blessing ordained by Christ, in which he himself, and God through him, confer the
supreme consecration and the plenitude of graces on earthly offerings" (op. cit.,
vol. 3, p. 185).

[2] Literally: "Make this coagulated milk holy by coagulating us to thy charity".

## Blessing for other offerings

In any blessing, say:

> Glory to thee, Father and Son,
> with the Holy Spirit,
> in the holy Church,[1]
> now and always
> and for ever and ever.
> > Amen.

## 7. Communion prayers [2]

Let the bishop say:

> We entreat you again, almighty God,
> Father of our Lord Jesus Christ:
> grant us to receive this holy mystery
> with blessing.
> Do not condemn anyone among us.

---

[1] The use in the doxology of the phrase "in the holy Church" is characteristic of the liturgy of Hippolytus (*Apostolic Tradition*, 3, 4, 6, 8, 22, 23). It is found again in an apocryphal prayer attributed to St Cyprian (see J. Lebreton, *Histoire du dogme de la Trinité*, Paris, 4th ed., vol. 2, p. 623). Without doubt it is inspired by Eph. 3, 21; Hippolytus could have taken it over direct from Irenaeus (N. Maurice-Denis and R. Boulet, *Eucharistie*, Paris, 1953, p. 375). Dom P. Cagin (*L'anaphore apostolique*. op. cit., p. 111) notes that it is a "studied liturgical use". Instead of expressing the equality of the Spirit with the Father and the Son as the traditional Latin doxology does, it underlines the special relation which unites the Spirit to the first two persons, as well as his role of sanctification "in the holy Church". The Church is thus the place of privilege where the holiness of God is diffused by the Spirit.

[2] The authenticity of these communion prayers is disputed: they are found only in the Ethiopian text of the *Egyptian Church Order*, though there are parallels to them in the *Apostolic Constitutions*. The question remains open (see Dom. B. Botte, *La Tradition apostolique*, op. cit., p. 35, n. 1).

Let all those who receive this holy mystery
be made worthy of the body and the blood of Christ,
almighty Lord, our God.

Let the deacon say:

Pray.

Let the bishop say:

Almighty God, make us to be strengthened
by receiving thy holy mystery.
Let it not condemn anyone among us
but bless us all through Christ.
Through him, glory to thee and power,
now and always
and for all eternity.
      Amen.

Let the deacon say:

You who are standing, bow your heads.

Let the bishop say:

Everliving God who knowest that which is hidden
and that which is revealed:
thy people bow their heads before thee,
breaking down the stubbornness of heart and flesh.
Look down from thy glorious dwelling on high.
Bless them, men and women together.
Incline thine ear to them.
Hear their prayer.
Strengthen them with thy mighty hand.
Protect them from every evil malady.

> Guard them body and soul.
> Increase in them and in us
> faith in thee, fear before thee,
> through thine only Son.
> Through him, glory to thee and power,
> with him and the Holy Spirit,
> now and always
> and for ever.
> > Amen.

Let the deacon then say:
> Attend.

Let the bishop say:
> Holy things to the holy!

Let the people say:
> One holy Father alone,
> one holy Son alone,
> one holy Spirit alone!

Let the bishop say:
> The Lord be with you.

Let the people reply:
> And with thy spirit.

Then let them raise their hands to give glory. Let the people draw near for the salvation of their souls. Let them communicate that their sins may be forgiven them.

Prayer after communion:

> Almighty God, Father of the Lord
> and our Saviour Jesus Christ,

we give thee thanks for having granted us
to receive thy holy mystery.
Let it not be a cause for us
of fault or of condemnation,
but let it renew soul, body and spirit,
through thine only Son.
Through him, glory to thee and power,
with him and the Holy Spirit,
now and always
and for ever.

And let the people reply:

Amen.

When they have communicated, let the priest lay his hands
on them and say:

Everliving, almighty God, Father of the Lord
and our Saviour Jesus Christ,
bless thy servants, men and women.
Protect them, uphold them,
content them by the power of thine archangel.
Guard them, strengthen in them
awe in the presence of thy majesty.
Give them peace without fear or anxiety,
through thine only Son.
Through him, glory to thee and power,
with him and the Holy Spirit
now and always
and for ever.

Let the people reply:

Amen.

Let the bishop say:
> The Lord be with you.

And let the people reply:
> And with thy spirit.

Let the deacon say:
> Go in peace.

With that the sacrifice is finished.

## 8. *Prayer for the ordination of priests*

When the bishop ordains a priest, let him lay his hand on the head of the ordinand, while the other priests too touch him.[1] Let him pronounce prayers like those which have been set down above, as for a bishop.

Let him make the following prayer:

> God and Father of our Lord Jesus Christ,
> cast thine eyes upon thy servant who is here.
> Grant to him the Spirit of grace and counsel,
> so that he may help the (other) priests
> and govern thy people with a pure heart.
>
> It was thus that thou didst cast thine eyes
> on the people whom thou didst choose,
> and that thou didst command Moses
> to choose elders:[2]

---

[1] The Roman ritual has kept this rite for the ordination of a priest: following the bishop all the priests present lay their hands on the ordinands.

[2] An allusion to the seventy elders who assisted Moses at the time the Covenant was made, Ex. 24, 1–11. The Greek text plays on the two meanings of *presbyteros* which can be translated either as "elder" or "priest".

thou didst fill them with thy Spirit
which thou didst give to thy servant.

And now, Lord, grant us
always to preserve in ourselves the Spirit of thy grace.
Make us worthy to serve thee with faith,
in simplicity of heart.

We praise thee through thy Child, Christ Jesus.
Through him, glory to thee and power,
Father and Son, with the Holy Spirit,
in the holy Church,
now and for ever and ever.
>           Amen.

## 9. *Prayer for deacons*

We command that only the bishop lay his hands on the
one to be ordained deacon. For a deacon is not ordained for the
priesthood, but for the service of the bishop, to carry out his
orders (. . .)

Let him say the following prayer over the deacon:

O God who didst create the universe
and didst order it by thy Word,
O Father of our Lord Jesus Christ
whom thou didst send to carry out thy will
and to manifest thy designs to us:
Grant the Spirit of grace,
of zeal and of diligence
to thy servant who is here.

Thou hast chosen him for the service of thy Church
and to bring into the Holy of Holies
the offering presented by the high priests[1]
that thou hast established for the glory of thy name.
Let him serve thee in this order,
without reproach and with purity.
Let him be found worthy, according to thy good
  pleasure,
to rise to a higher degree.
Let him praise thee through thy Son Jesus Christ,
  our Lord.
Through him, glory to thee, power and honour,
with the Holy Spirit,
now, always and for ever.
  Amen.

## *10. The forms of liturgical prayer*

(. . .) Let the bishop give thanks in the manner described
above. It is not, however, necessary for him to use the form of
words set out there, as though he had to make the effort to say
them by heart in his thanksgiving to God.[2]

Let each pray according to his abilities. If a man can make
a becoming and worthy prayer, it is well. But if he prays in a
different way, and yet with moderation, you must not prevent
him, provided that the prayer is correct and conforms to
orthodoxy.

---

[1] The deacon presented to the bishop the offering with which the eucharist
was celebrated. See the *Apostolic Tradition*, 4 and 23, p. 38 and 62.

[2] Hippolytus again bears witness to the bishop's freedom to improvise liturgical
prayer on the basis of a typical schema, provided that the prayer "conformed to
orthodoxy". From the fourth century on, the rule was to use texts which had
already been fixed by tradition. Exceptions, however, lingered in certain liturgies
until the seventh century. See J. A. Jungmann, *Missarum Solemnia*, op. cit., vol. 1,
p. 56, n. 10.

## 12. The reader

When someone is ordained reader, let the bishop hand him the book. Let him not lay his hands on him.

## 13. Virgins

Concerning virgins: A virgin does not receive the laying on of hands; it is her choice alone that makes her a virgin.

## 14. Subdeacons

As for subdeacons: Subdeacons do not receive the laying on of hands: but they are appointed to serve the deacon.

# Second Part

### Christian initiation

## 16. The admission of catechumens

The second part of Hippolytus' *Apostolic Tradition* deals with the catechumenate and with baptism.[1]

What we learn about the catechumenate such as it was in the Roman community at the beginning of the third century will not fail

---

[1] For the history of the catechumenate, see A. Stenzel, *Die Taufe*, Innsbruck, 1958; M. Dujarier, "l'Évolution de la pastorale du catéchuménat aux six premiers siècles de l'Église", *Maison-Dieu*, 71, pp. 46–61.

to surprise the Church historian or even the ordinary Christian of today. For, although the Church was in the full flood of expansion, there is nowhere any trace to be found of organised activity or of any kind of propaganda. She gave proof of intense missionary labour but had no missionaries, at least in the sense of members of the clergy specially set apart for the task of evangelisation. She continually confronted and conquered the paganism by which she was surrounded, and yet had no workers specially trained for the task.

The explanation of this missionary "miracle" is of course first to be found in the dynamic character of the message of Christ and in the action of the Holy Spirit on the souls of men, but we cannot omit either the missionary witness which each Christian bore to the faith which he had received. The Church was missionary without having "missionaries", because each and every one of her members was truly an apostle. Reflecting on this marvellous expansion of Christianity in the first three centuries, Harnack wrote: "The missionaries of the Christian religion who were most numerous and had the greatest success were not those whose profession was to teach, but the Christians themselves in the measure in which they were faithful and strong. . . . It was characteristic of this religion that every adherent who professed it seriously propagated it. Christians had to let their light shine so that the pagans, seeing their good works, might glorify the Father in heaven. When they were convinced of their business and lived according to the precepts of their religion, they simply could not remain hidden: their life itself had to be a missionary preaching both clear and startling."[1]

Thus Hippolytus has no word to describe priests or other members of the clergy who recruited catechumens, but speaks readily of "those who introduce them".[2] Every member of the community fulfilled his apostolic task in virtue of baptism itself by which he was deputed to this mission.

It is also worth drawing attention to the severity which was shown in the choice of candidates for baptism. Evidently the Church preferred not to grow numerically rather than to diminish in quality. She excluded from the catechumenate not only those whose professions

---

[1] A. von Harnack, *Die Mission und Ausbreitung des Christentums in den ersten drei Jahrhunderten*, 4th ed., 1924, vol. 1, p. 377 f.

[2] See 16 and 20, p. 52 and p. 55.

were manifestly opposed to the law of God, such as brothel-keepers and prostitutes, idolatrous priests, wizards, sorcerers and fortune-tellers, but also those whose professional activities were exercised on the frontier of sin. In an age when all social life was impregnated with paganism, this frontier was broad and vague enough. Hippolytus excludes from the catechumenate the sculptors or painters who furnished the dying paganism with idols, actors, since the theatre of the age was bound up with immorality, the performers in the circus who toyed with human life, the gladiators who exposed themselves to butchery, the magistrates who had to organise pagan festivals and orgies. Soldiers were accepted only with hesitation, since they had to take oaths and the armies of that age were not exactly schools of virtue.

This primitive severity in regard to catechumens honours the Church. It was not hostility to sinners but to sin.

Those who are to be initiated into the new faith must first be brought to the catechists[1] to hear the word, before the people arrive.

They are to be asked their reasons for seeking the faith.

Those who introduce them will bear witness in their regard in order that it may be known whether they are capable of hearing the Word. Their state of life also is to be scrutinised (. . .).

Enquiry is to be made about the trades and professions of those who are brought for instruction.

If a man is a procurer, that is to say, supports prostitutes, let him give it up or be sent away.

If he is a sculptor or painter, he is to be instructed not to make any more idols. Let him give it up or be sent away.

If he is an actor or gives performances in the theatre, let him give it up or be sent away.

---

[1] Literally "doctors".

If he teaches children, it is preferable that he should give it up.[1] But if he has no trade, he is to be allowed to continue.

If he is a charioteer, a wrestler or attends wrestling matches, let him give it up or be sent away.

If he is gladiator, or teaches gladiators to fight, or a hunter,[2] or if he is a public official who organises the gladiatorial games, let him give it up or be sent away.

If he is a priest of idols or a guardian of idols, let him give it up or be sent away.

A soldier who is in a position of authority is not to be allowed to put anyone to death; if he is ordered to, he is not to do it, he is not to be allowed to take an oath. If he does not accept these conditions, he is to be sent away.

A man who has the power of the sword, or magistrate of a city who wears the purple; let him give it up or be sent away.

Catechumens or believers who want to enlist as soldiers are to be sent away, for they have treated God with contempt.

A prostitute, or a pederast, or a man who has mutilated himself, or one who has committed the unspeakable thing, are to be sent away, for they are defiled.

Wizards too are not to be admitted as candidates.

Sorcerers, astrologers, fortune-tellers, interpreters of dreams, coiners,[3] makers of amulets must give up these activities: otherwise they are to be sent away.

---

[1] Teachers or professors were charged with explaining mythology to their pupils.

[2] This must mean one who furnished wild beasts for the games in the circus.

[3] The text here is dubious. The passage is corrupt. Botte (*La Tradition apostolique*, Münster, 1963, p. 39) proposes to translate it: "the trickster, the 'cutter' who cuts pieces (of money)".

If a concubine who is the slave of some man has brought up her children and is living only with this man, she is to be admitted; otherwise she is to be sent away.

A man who has a concubine is to give her up and take a wife according to the law. If he refuses he is to be sent away.

If we have omitted anything, make a suitable decision yourselves. For we all have the Spirit of God.[1]

## 17. *The three-year catechumenate*

The catechumen is to attend the instruction for three years.

However, if a man shows himself zealous and really perseveres in this undertaking, you are to judge him not by length of time but by his conduct.

## 18-19. *The instruction*[2]

When the catechist has finished his instruction, the catechumens are to pray by themselves, apart from the faithful.

After the prayer, the catechist is to lay his hands on them while he says a prayer. Whether he is of the clergy or the laity, he is to do this.

## *Baptism of blood*

If a catechumen is thrown into prison for the name of God,

---

[1] A golden rule—every bishop possesses the Holy Spirit and can trust in him when deciding difficult cases for which no precedent exists.

[2] The "catechism lesson" was not merely instruction; it began with prayer and ended with the blessing given by the catechist, who laid his hands on them.

he is not to be left in doubt as to his witness. For indeed, if he
suffers violence and is put to death before he has received pardon
for his sins, he will be justified nevertheless, for he is baptised
in his own blood.[1]

## 20. *Preparatory Rites for Baptism*

### Choosing the candidates

When those who are to be baptised have been chosen, their
life is to be examined—whether they have lived devoutly during
their catechumenate, whether they have respected widows,
visited the sick, practised all the other good works.[2]

### The giving of the Gospel

If those who introduce them bear witness that they have
been living in this way, let them hear the Gospel.[3]

---

[1] In his treatise *On Baptism* Tertullian attests the same belief for the African
Church: "We have also a second baptism, it too unique, the baptism of blood which
the Lord said he had to receive (Lk. 12, 50), even though he was already baptised.
He had come, that is,, 'through water and through blood' (I Jn. 5, 6), through water
to be baptised, and through blood to be glorified. That is why he has made us
through water 'called' and through blood 'chosen'. These two baptisms gushed
together from the wound in his pierced side. . . . This second baptism takes the
place of the baptism of water when a man has not received it, and restores it to him
when he has lost it" (*On Baptism*, 16, 1-2; *P.L.* 1, 1217 AB; *Corpus Christianorum,
Series Latina*, 1, pp. 290-291). Elsewhere, speaking of martyrs, Tertullian writes:
"It is your blood that is the key of paradise" (*On the Soul*, 55, 5; *P.L.* 2, 745 A;
*Corpus Christianorum, Series Latina*, 1, p. 863).

[2] Note that the examination of the candidates is concerned not with the
knowledge they have acquired but with the life they have led.

[3] The preceding instructions were doubtless concerned in a general way with
the principles of Christian living. From the *traditio* (giving over, handing down)
of the Gospel, the teaching concentrated more directly on the proclamation of the
Good News of salvation.

## *The daily exorcisms*

From the moment when they have been chosen, they are to undergo exorcisms every day by the imposition of hands.

As the day of their baptism approaches, the bishop is to exorcise each of them, to find out if they are pure. If there is one among them who is not, he is to be rejected, for he has not heard the Word with faith, because the (demon) stranger remains always hidden in him (. . .).[1]

## *Fasting and prayer*

Those who are to be baptised must fast on the Friday and the Saturday.

On the Saturday, the bishop gathers them all together in one place and bids them all pray and kneel.[2]

As he lays his hands on them, let him conjure all the foreign spirits to depart from them and never to return to them again.

## *The baptismal vigil*

When he has finished the exorcism, let him breathe upon their faces,[3] make the sign on their ears and nose and then bid

---

[1] The text is obscure. Funk (*Didascalia*, op. cit., vol. 2, p. 108) proposes to read: "Quia impossibile est, alienum in aeternum occultum manere", "because it is impossible for the stranger to remain hidden for ever".

[2] Tertullian writes similarly: "Those who wish to approach baptism must pray frequently with fasts, genuflections and vigils. To this they are to add the confession of all their past sins, in memory of the baptism of John; they were baptised, we are told, confessing their sins" (*On Baptism*, 20, 1; *P.L.* 1, 1222 BC; *Corpus Christianorum, Series Latina*, 1, p. 294).

[3] The rite of exsufflation is a rite of exorcism intended to drive away the devil. It is distinguished from the rite of insufflation which symbolises the gift of the Holy Spirit and which Christ himself performed for the apostles (Jn. 20, 22).

them rise and keep watch through the night. They are to be given readings and instructions.

Those to be baptised are to bring no vessel with them other than the one they must bring for the Eucharist,[1] it is fitting that he who is worthy of it should make the offering.

### 21. *The giving of holy baptism*

## *They are to come to the pure water*

At cockcrow, they are to come to the water; this must be running water and pure.

They are to take off their clothes.

The children are baptised first. All those who can, are to reply for themselves. If they cannot, let their parents reply for them, or another member of the family.[2]

Next you baptise the men, then the women; the women will have unbound their hair and taken off their jewels of gold and silver.

No one is to go down into the water with anything of the stranger.[3]

## *The oil of thanksgiving and the oil of exorcism*

At the time appointed for the baptism, the bishop says a prayer of thanksgiving over the oil and collects it in a vessel. It is this oil which is called "oil of thanksgiving".

---

[1] This must mean to carry the eucharist home.

[2] This text bears witness to the practice of infant baptism in the Roman Church. On this matter see J. Jeremias, *Die Kindertaufe in den ersten vier Jahrhunderten*, Göttingen, 1958.

[3] This must mean anything which belongs to "the stranger", i.e., the devil.

Next he takes another oil and pronounces an exorcism over it; this oil is called "oil of exorcism".

The deacon carries the oil of exorcism and stands on the left of the priest. Another deacon takes the oil of thanksgiving and stands on the right of the priest.

## Renunciation of Satan

The priest takes each of those who are to receive baptism aside. He orders each to turn towards the West and to swear in these terms:

> I renounce thee, Satan,
> and all thine undertakings
> and all thy works.

## The anointing of exorcism

After this renunciation, he gives them an anointing with the oil of exorcism, saying:

Let every evil spirit depart far from thee.

Then he leads them back to the bishop or to the priest, who is standing near the water of baptism. A deacon goes down into the water with the one who is going to be baptised.

## The triple immersion

This latter goes down into the water. He who is baptising him lays his hand on his head and asks him:

> Dost thou believe in God,
> the almighty Father?

The one who is being baptised replies: "I believe".

Then he baptises him the first time, keeping his hand laid on his head.

Next he asks him:

> Dost thou believe in Christ Jesus,
> the Son of God,
> born by the Holy Spirit of the Virgin Mary,
> who died and was buried,
> who rose again on the third day,
> living from among the dead,
> who ascended into heaven,
> who sits at the right hand of the Father,
> who will come to judge the living and the dead?

When he replies: "I believe", he baptises him a second time.

He asks him again:

> Dost thou believe in the Holy Spirit,
> in the Holy Church,
> in the resurrection of the flesh?

He who is being baptised replies: "I believe". Then he is baptised a third time.[1]


## The anointing with the oil of thanksgiving

After that he comes up again. Then the priest gives him an anointing with the oil which has been sanctified.[2] He says:

---

[1] Note that the *Apostolic Tradition* does not contain the traditional baptisma formula, inherited from Mt. 28, 19: "I baptise thee in the name of the Father and of the Son and of the Holy Spirit." At that time the triple question and the triple profession of faith in the Father, the Son and the Spirit took the place of a baptismal formula.

[2] This anointing corresponds to the postbaptismal anointing with holy chrism

I anoint thee with the oil which has been sanctified
in the name of Jesus Christ.

After they have dried themselves, they put on their clothes
again and go into the church.

### Confirmation

According to the *Apostolic Tradition*, the ceremonies of confirmation include a laying on of hands by the bishop, with a prayer of
deprecation, an anointing with the oil of thanksgiving, the making of
a sign on the forehead and the kiss of peace.

Confirmation took place immediately after baptism. We know
that in the East the two sacraments, baptism and confirmation, were
given simultaneously, sometimes by the same rites. At Rome and in
the West, they were administered in two different rites, as Hippolytus
witnesses and Pope Innocent I was later to sanction,[1] but at one and
the same ceremony.[2]

## 22. The laying on of hands

As he lays his hands on them, the bishop invokes (God)
saying:

---

in our present ritual (*Ordo baptismi adultorum*, 41; see R. Béraudy, *L'initiation chrétienne*, in A. G. Martimort, *L'Église en prière*, Paris, 1961, pp. 542–546). It signifies that
the one baptised has become a *Christian*, that is to say a sharer in *Christ*, pre-eminently
the Anointed One. Tertullian explains: "When we have come out of the bath, we
receive an anointing with blessed oil, following the ancient usage. . . . And our
name 'christ' comes from 'chrisma' which means anointing and also gives its
name to the Lord" (*On Baptism*, 7, 1; *P.L.* 1, 1206C–1207A; *Corpus Christianorum,
Series Latina*, 1, p. 282; see also R. F. Refoulé and M. Drouzy, *Tertullien, Traité
du baptême*, Sources chrétiennes, 35, Paris, 1952, p. 76).

[1] *Letter to Decennius*, 19 March, 416; *P.L.* 20, 554B; B. Mansi, *Sacrorum
conciliorum nova et amplissima collectio*, 3, 1029BC.

[2] It was only from the ninth century on that in the West the administration of
confirmation was frequently separated from that of baptism. See R. Béraudy,
*L'initiation chrétienne*, op. cit., pp. 552–560.

> Lord God,
> who hast given to these the dignity
> of meriting the remission of their sins
> through the bath of regeneration of the Holy Spirit,
> fill them with thy grace
> that they may serve thee according to thy will.
> For to thee is the glory,
> Father and Son, with the Holy Spirit
> in the holy Church,
> now and for ever and ever.
>    Amen.

## The anointing

Next, with his hand, he pours out the blessed oil. He puts it on their heads saying:

> I give thee the anointing with the blessed oil,
> in the Lord God, the almighty Father,
> Christ Jesus and the Holy Spirit.

## The seal of the Holy Spirit

Next he marks them with the sign on the forehead,[1] then he gives them a kiss saying:

> The Lord is with thee.

He who has been marked with the sign replies:

> And with thy spirit.

This is to be done for each of them.

---

[1] The Latin here uses the word *signare*. In Christian vocabulary *signare* means to stamp with a seal (A. Blaise and H. Chirat, *Dictionnaire latin-français des auteurs chrétiens*, 1945). Here we have to do with the rite which symbolises the spiritual seal conferred on the soul by the Holy Spirit.

From then on they are to pray with the whole people. But they are not to pray with the faithful until they have received all this.

When they have prayed, let them give the kiss of peace.

### 23. *The baptismal mass and first communion*

## *The offering*

Then the deacons present the offering to the bishop.

He blesses the bread which represents the body of Christ; the chalice in which the wine is mixed, which represents the blood poured out for all those who believe in him; the milk and honey[1] mixed together, to signify the fulfilment of the promise which (God) made to our fathers, signified by the land flowing with milk and honey, realised by the flesh of Christ which he gives us, by which the believers are nourished like little children,[2] for the sweetness of his word changes the bitterness of our hearts to gentleness; lastly, the water for the offering, to signify purification, so that the inward man who is spiritual may receive the same effect as the body.

The bishop is to explain all this carefully to all who receive it.

---

[1] The custom of offering milk and honey to the newly baptised was still observed in Rome at the beginning of the sixth century, as we learn from John the Deacon (John the Deacon, *Letter to Senarius*, 12; P.L. 59, 405C–406A).

[2] An allusion to I Peter 2, 2: "Like new-born children desire the spiritual milk without fraud, in order that through him (that is, through the Lord) you may grow up to salvation."

## *Communion*

Having broken the bread, he distributes each morsel saying:

> The bread of heaven
> in Christ Jesus!

He who receives it replies: "Amen".

If there are not sufficient priests present, let the deacons also offer the cups. They are to stand in an orderly manner and modestly, the first to present the water, the second the milk, and the third the wine.

Those who are drinking take a little from each cup, while the one presenting it says:

> In God, the almighty Father.

He who receives it replies: "Amen".

> And in the Lord Christ,
> in the Holy Spirit
> and in the holy Church.

He replies: "Amen". This is to be done for each of them.

When this is finished, each hastens to do good works, to please God and live a good life.[1] He is to devote himself to the Church, putting what he has been taught into practice and making progress in the service of God.

---

[1] According to Christian tradition, participation in the eucharist necessarily implies that the believer commits himself to a more complete fulfilment of the demands of Christian living. See J. Lécuyer, *Le Sacrifice de la Nouvelle Alliance*, 1962, pp. 232–240, especially pp. 237–238.

# *Third Part*

## *Christian observances*

The third part of the *Apostolic Tradition* deals with various observances of Christian living. Hippolytus tells us about the Agape meal, the Lucernary office, offerings presented for the bishop's blessing, the reception of the eucharist at home, the duty of deacons and priests, the hours more specially consecrated to prayer, the maintenance of cemeteries and the sign of the cross. Thus we have a vivid picture of the devotions of the first Christians. Their piety, enlivened by the community celebration of the eucharist, overflowed the structure of the liturgical assembly and affected their whole life. In these years when the persecutions were still intermittent and had not come to a definite end, the Christians, wholeheatedly and joyfully, followed the Lord's command: "Watch and pray at all times . . . in order that you may appear with confidence before the Son of Man."[1]

## 26. The *Agape*[2]

When the bishop eats with the rest of the faithful, each guest receives a morsel of bread from his hand before breaking his own. This is a "eulogy"[3] and not the eucharist like the body of the Lord.

Before drinking, each, as he takes a cup, is to give thanks. Then eat and drink, after you have been purified, you who are present and receiving your meal in this way (. . .)

---

[1] Lk. 21, 36.

[2] In Christian vocabulary the Greek word *agape* (charity) signifies an evening meal given by a member of the community, especially for the poor and for widows.

[3] In liturgical language, "eulogy" (from the Greek *eulogia*) means the little loaves which were blessed and then given to those who had offered them or shared out among those present.

## 27. *The Lucernary*

On Saturday evening, the beginning of the vigil of the Lord's day, the faithful were accustomed to come together for an evening of prayer, called Lucernary.[1] A lamp was lit in memory of the risen Christ, splendour of the Father's glory and light of the world,[2] and in expectation of the Parousia. Hippolytus describes this ancient office, which had become the daily evening prayer for the whole Christian community.

When evening falls and the bishop has arrived, the deacon brings a lamp. Standing in the midst of the faithful, the bishop begins to give thanks, saluting them to start with saying:

> The Lord be with you!

And all the people reply:

> And with thy spirit!

(Then the bishop says:)

> Let us give thanks to the Lord.

They reply:

> It is worthy and just.
> To him greatness and magnificence
> as well as glory.

He does not say: "Let us lift up our hearts", because that is said at the moment of the offering.[3]

---

[1] In Greek *lychnikon*, that is, Office of the Light. The lighting of the upper room at Troas where Paul presided over the breaking of bread on a Saturday evening bears witness to the celebration of the first "lucernaries". On the rite of lucernaries, see Schuster, *Liber sacramentorum*, Brussels, vol. 4, *L'Eucharistia lucernaris*, pp. 7–22. The Roman liturgy has kept some of the elements of the ancient Lucernary in the Paschal Vigil (Blessing of fire, of incense, singing of the Exultet or laus ceraei; see L. Bouyer, *Le Mystère paschal*, Lex Orandi 4, 5th ed., Paris, 1957, pp. 381–4c1).

[2] Heb. 1, 3; Jn. 8, 12.

[3] See p. 38.

Then let him pray like this:

> We give thee thanks, O God,
> through thy Son, our Lord Jesus Christ,
> for having enlightened us
> by revealing to us the incorruptible light.
> Having finished the course of this day,
> arrived at the verge of night,
> filled with the light of the day
> which thou didst create for our joy,
> now that we do not lack
> light for the evening,
> we sanctify thee and glorify thee
> through thine only Son, our Lord Jesus Christ.

> It is through him and with him that thou hast
> glory, power and honour,
> now and for ever and ever.
> Amen.

Then everyone replies: "Amen".

After they have risen from the meal and the children and the virgins have prayed, they recite some psalms (. . .)[1]

## 28. *The offering of fruit and flowers*

The faithful liked to present the first of the fruit they had picked, as well as roses and lilies, for the blessing of the bishop. These offerings

---

[1] The traditional psalm for the Lucernary was Ps. 141, the second verse of which seemed especially suitable: "Let my prayer rise before thee like incense, and my hands like the evening offering". "Joyous Light" was sung for a hymn (see *Hymnes et prières*, Vivante Tradition 2, p. 131), with the refrain: "We sing the Father and the Son and the Holy Spirit of God" (see St Basil of Caesarea, *Treatise on the Holy Ghost*, 29; *P.G.* 32, 205A; B. Pruche, *Basile de Césarée, Traité du Saint Esprit*, Sources chrétiennes 17, Paris, 1945, p. 250).

recall to some extent the offering of first-fruits in the Old Testament. In offering fruit, roses and lilies the believer celebrated the goodness of God who had given them to him. He read the name of God in the fruits of the earth, and God read the homage of love in the heart of the man who offered them.

When the fruit has appeared and the picking has begun, everyone hastens to bring some of it to the bishop. When he offers it, he blesses it, naming those who have brought it and saying:

> We give thee thanks, O God,
> and offer thee the first of the fruit
> which thou hast given us to enjoy.

> By thy word, thou hast made them grow,
> thou hast ordained that the earth should bear all the fruit
> for the joy and the nourishment
> of men and of all the animals.

> For all this we praise thee, O God,
> and for the succour thou givest
> by adorning the whole creation
> with all kinds of fruit,
> through thy Child Jesus Christ, our Lord.

> Through him, glory to thee
> for ever and ever,
>       Amen.

The following fruits are blessed: grapes, figs, pomegranates, olives, pears, apples, mulberries, peaches, cherries, almonds, plums; not melons, watermelons, cucumbers, mushrooms, garlic, nor any other vegetable. But sometimes flowers are offered too; thus roses and lilies are offered, but no other flowers.

Everything that is harvested, holy God is to be thanked for, and it is to be used for his glory.

### 30. *The duty of deacons and sub-deacons*

All deacons, as well as the sub-deacons, are to attend eagerly on the bishop.

The bishop is also to be informed who is ill, so that, if he judges it to be fitting, he may visit them. For it gives great pleasure to the sick man, if the high priest is mindful of him.

### 32. *Communion in the home*

Every believer, before tasting other food, is to take care to receive the Eucharist. For if he receives it with faith, even if afterwards he is given something poisonous, it will not be able to do him harm.

Everyone is to take care that no unbeliever, no mouse or other animal[1] eats of the Eucharist, and that no particle of the Eucharist falls on the ground or is lost. For it is the body of the Lord that the faithful eat and it is not to be treated carelessly (. . .)

### 34. *Cemeteries*

A heavy charge is not to be imposed on people for burying their dead in the cemeteries, for it is the affair of all the poor.

---

[1] This prudential advice is explained by the fact that the Christians kept the eucharist by them, at home. The custom of keeping the eucharist at home is also attested by Tertullian (*Ad uxorem*, 11, 5; *P.L.* 1, 1295A–1297A; *Corpus Christianorum, Series Latina*, 1, pp. 389–390: *De oratione*, 19; *P.L.* 1, 1183A; *Corpus Christianorum, Series Latina*, 1, pp. 267–268); it survived until about the eighth century, as a text of the Venerable Bede (673–735) in his *Ecclesiastical History* witnesses, 4, 24 (*P.L.* 95, 214CD).

However, the wages of the gravedigger and the price of the bricks are to be regulated. The bishop is to support those who are settled there and work there, so that they do not become a burden to the families of the dead.[1]

## 35. *The hours of prayer*

### *In the morning*

All the faithful, men and women, when they wake from sleep in the morning, before undertaking any kind of work, are to wash their hands[2] and pray to God. Then they go to their work.

### *Word of God and community prayer*

However, if there is an instruction on the Word of God, everyone will go to it gladly, with this thought in his mind, that it is God whom he hears speaking through the mouth of the man giving the instruction. For if he has prayed in the assembly, he is ready to overcome the evil of the day.

The man who fears God holds it a great loss not to go thither where the instruction is given, above all if he knows how to read.

On the arrival of the one who is to teach, let none among you be tardy in joining the assembly, in the place where the instruction is given. The speaker will teach what is useful for all, and you, you will hear things that you have forgotten, you will draw profit from what the Holy Spirit gives you through the teacher. Thus your faith will be strengthened by what you have heard. You will

---

[1] "To the families of the dead", literally "to him who comes there".

[2] A rite of purification (Ps. 26, 6) which signifies that the soul, before entering into the presence of God, rids itself of its imperfections and faults.

be told there, too, what you ought to do at home. Everyone then is to be careful to go to the assembly, for the Holy Spirit acts with power there.

On a day when there is no instruction, everyone is to take a holy book in his own home and read enough from it of what is useful to him.

## *At the third hour*

If you are at home at the third hour, pray and praise God.[1] But if at that moment you find yourself elsewhere, pray to God in your heart. For it was at that hour that Christ was nailed to the wood. This is why, in the Old Testament, the Law laid down that they should offer continually the loaves of proposition[2] which symbolised the body and blood of Christ, and sacrifice a lamb devoid of reason, which symbolised the perfect Lamb. It is Christ, indeed, who is the shepherd; and he is also the bread come down from heaven.

## *At the sixth hour*

Similarly, pray at the sixth hour. For while Christ was fixed to the wood, that day's course was arrested and great darkness rose. So at that hour make a prayer of great power, in imitation of him who prayed then, while the whole of creation was plunged into darkness on account of the unbelief of the Jews.

---

[1] The third, sixth and ninth hours correspond to 9 a.m., midday and 3 p.m. The practice of praying three times a day was certainly inherited from Old Testament piety (Ps. 55; Dan. 6, 11). The usage passed into the Christian community, as the *Didache* (8) already shows (see *Les Pères apostoliques*, Vivante Tradition, 1, pp. 15–16).

[2] The loaves of proposition were twelve cakes of the best flour which were set out in the "Holy Place" and were renewed every sabbath (see Lev. 24, 5–9; 1 Chr. 9, 32; 23, 29). The text of Num. 4, 7 calls them "the loaves of the perpetual offering".

## At the ninth hour

At the ninth hour lengthen out your prayer and praise greatly, in imitation of the souls of the just who bless God, the true God who remembered his holy ones and sent his Son, the Word, to enlighten them.

For it was at this hour that the water and the blood flowed from the pierced side of Christ and that (the Lord) gave light to the declining day and brought it to evening. Thus, by beginning a new day[1] at the hour when he began to fall asleep,[2] he gave us an image of the resurrection.

## In the evening

Similarly pray before your body goes to take its rest in bed.

## Nocturnal praise

Towards the middle of the night,[3] rise, wash your hands with water and pray.

If your wife is present, pray both of you together. If, however, she is not a believer, withdraw to another room to pray, then return to bed.

---

[1] Hippolytus is reckoning the day in the semitic manner; Saturday, the "new day", then, begins on Friday evening, not at midnight.

[2] Hippolytus means Christ's death.

[3] Nocturnal prayer is an inheritance from Judaism: "I rise in the middle of the night, giving thee thanks for thy judgments" (Ps. 119, 62). It is found also in the Qumran texts (Rule, 10, 10 and 14): "When day and night come, I will enter into the Alliance of God, and when evening and morning withdraw, I will tell his precepts. . . . When I go to my bed, I will cry out to him with joy" (See A. Dupont-Sommer, *Les Écrits esséniens découverts près de la Mer Morte*, Paris, 1959, pp 113–114; J. Carmignac and P. Guilbert, *Les Textes de Qumrân*, Paris, 1961, pp. 70 and 72).

Do not be idle in this matter of prayer (. . .)

When you breathe into your hands and sign yourself with the damp breath you have gathered, your body is purified right to the feet.[1] For the gift of the Spirit and the purification of water, which rise from the heart as from a spring, purify the believer who offers them.

At that hour then you should pray. For the men of old who bequeathed us this tradition taught us that at that hour the whole of creation rests for a moment to praise the Lord. The stars, the trees and the rivers stop for an instant, and the whole army of angels celebrates and praises God at that hour, with the souls of the just. This is why believers hasten to pray at that hour. The Lord himself bears witness to it when he says: "Behold, in the middle of the night a cry resounded, saying: It is the bridegroom coming! rise and go to meet him!" And he ended: "Watch therefore, for you do not know at what hour he is coming".[2]

## At cockcrow

Towards cockcrow, likewise rise. It was at this hour, while the cock crowed, that the sons of Israel denied Christ, him whom we know by faith, in whom we hope for the everlasting light for the resurrection of the dead, our eyes fixed on that day.

---

[1] The breath of the Christian has been sanctified by the *Breath* of God, that is by the Holy *Spirit* who dwells in the heart of the faithful. In signing himself, so to speak, with the Spirit of God, the believer is purified through and through.

[2] Mt. 25, 6, 13. The way in which the New Testament insists that the return of Jesus will take place during the night is well-known: Lk. 12, 20; 12, 39-40 and Mt. 24, 42-43; Lk. 17, 34 and Mt. 24, 40-41; Mt. 25, 1-13; Mk. 13, 35-37; I Thess. 5, 2. These texts seem to echo a hope attested by the Palestinian Targum, which placed the future messianic deliverance in the night of Passover (cf. Jer. 38, 8, *LXX*), which had become the central night of the whole history of the world and was associated with the night of creation and of the sacrifice of Abraham. See R. Le Déaut and J. Lécuyer, art. "Exode" in *Dict. de Spiritualité*, 4, 1966.

If all of you, the faithful, act in this way, if you keep it in mind, instructing each other, giving an example to the catechumens, you will be able neither to be tempted nor to be lost, since you have Christ always in mind.

### 36. *The sign of the Cross*

At all times be ready to sign yourselves carefully on the forehead. For this sign shows forth the Passion which opposes the devil, if you make it with faith, not to please men, but knowing how to use it like a breastplate. Thus the adversary, seeing the power of the Spirit which comes from the heart, flies as soon as you show this spiritual likeness outwardly. It is not you who inspire fear in him, but the Spirit who dwells in you. This is what Moses represented through the Passover lamb which was sacrificed, when he sprinkled the thresholds and smeared the doorposts with its blood. It denoted the faith which we now have in the perfect Lamb.

When we make the sign on our forehead and our eyes, we drive away him who seeks to destroy us.

### 37. *Conclusion*

If then these instructions are received with grace and right faith, they bring edification for the Church and everlasting life for believers (. . .)

Beloved, if we have left anything out, God will reveal it to those who are worthy. For he directs the holy Church so that she may arrive at the harbour of peace.

# 5

# The Didascalia of the Apostles
*(beginning of the third century)*

# Introduction

## The work

The *Didascalia* or *Catholic Teaching of the Twelve Apostles and the Holy Disciples of Our Saviour* is an ecclesiastical Constitution which dates from the first half, perhaps even from the first decades, of the third century.[1] Its author was a bishop in northern Syria. The work presents itself as a manual or custom-book for the use of the Christian community issued from paganism.

To give more weight and authority to the teaching and the rules which he formulates, the author does not hesitate to present his work as being that of the apostles and the immediate disciples of Christ himself. An affirmation like this can no longer surprise or excite the scholars of today and the writer's stratagem is easily unmasked. Indeed, the author himself betrays it by his use and exploitation of the *Didache*, the apocryphal *Gospel of Peter*, the apocryphal *Acts of Paul*, Ignatius of Antioch and Irenaeus. At that time such literary fictions were current practice; they were looked on with indulgence, even complicity, and did not offend the conscience of their readers, still less those of their authors, as long as they served the good cause. What was important above all was, in the best sense of the word, to edify the Christian community, to give it rules of life and to protect it too from the doctrinal and moral deviations which were always possible. It was thought that you could create an authentically Christian work, even through a literary fiction. Authenticity was looked for not on the part of the author but in the spirit of his work.

Thus it is that today, thanks to a forgery, we have the good fortune to be able to grasp the essentials of a Christian community at the beginning of the third century, to see with admiration how the spirit of the Gospel, with its dazzling charity, had penetrated the life of the clergy and the faithful, and to perceive the astonishing sense of community those Christians had, a sense so strong that they could say

---

[1] On the date, see P. Galtier, "La Date de la Didascalie des Apôtres" in *Revue d'histoire ecclésiastique*, 42 (1947), pp. 315-351.

77

that to fail to attend the assembly was to deprive Christ of one of his members and to rend the body of the Lord.[1] We come upon the bishop in the act of welcoming a poor man into his church and making him sit on the episcopal throne while he himself sits on the ground.[2] We see the deacons and deaconesses extending the ministry of the hierarchy in their respective fields;[3] we hear the magnificent penitential "Prayer of Manasseh",[4] we learn that each individual church must be a community of forgiveness and love.[5] "The more one studies the *Didascalia of the Apostles*", notes P. Galtier,[6] "the more apparent become its interest and importance." Harnack saw in it a "document unique in its own kind and of priceless worth."[7] No other exists which helps us to penetrate so intimately into the life of a church in the third century. . . . It allows us to follow the bishop in his work of teaching, directing and governing. We can see him entering into all the details of the life of his people. Surrounded by his clergy, he is its pastor, leader and judge. His regard extends and must extend to each and every one. Sinners and faithful alike are the object of his care. He has charge of their souls; but he provides also for their bodily needs."

## The plan of the work

The author has not tied himself down to a plan whose logic, to his way of thinking at least, would have overreached the needs of the subject he envisaged. To tell the truth, he deals with the subjects as they present themselves to his mind, taking considerable liberty, but at the same time skilfully avoiding too frequent repetitions.

In default of a plan in the strict sense of the word, the principal matters can be enumerated. Having given some instructions for married people (ch. 2-3), the author sets out the qualities and duties

---

[1] Ch. 13; see p. 91.
[2] Ch. 12; see p. 91.
[3] Ch. 16; see pp. 92-96.
[4] Ch. 7; see p. 83.
[5] Ch. 6; see p. 80.
[6] From the article quoted above, p. 77, n. 1.
[7] *Die Mission und Ausbreitung des Christentums*, 3rd ed., Leipzig, 1915, Vol. 2, p. 157—reference given by P. Galtier.

of the bishop (ch. 4; he comes back to this subject in ch. 7-9 and 11-12). Then he considers penitence and the pardon of sinners (ch. 6), and shows himself clearly to be milder than his western contemporaries Tertullian, Hippolytus and Cyprian. Next we learn what the qualities and duties of deacons are (ch. 11 and 16), and the good order that is to be kept in the assembly of the faithful (ch. 13). He goes on to deal with widows (ch. 14-15), deaconesses (ch. 16), the education of the young and of orphans (ch. 17 and 22), the resurrection of the dead (ch. 20), heresies and schisms (ch. 23), the apostles and the Church (ch. 24-25), and the abolition of the rules of legal purity laid down in the book of Deuteronomy (ch. 25). As can be seen, the plan followed is in no way rigid and does not lack a certain element of whimsicality.

On one's way through the book, one comes across plenty of biblical quotations adorning it, some of which are very long. Plainly the author of the *Didascalia* knew and loved the Word of God and took pleasure in using it to support his own words.

## Textual tradition

The *Didascalia* was written in Greek. Apart from some short fragments, this original version is lost. But it is possible to reconstitute the greater part of it thanks to the *Apostolic Constitutions*, the first six chapters of which are an exact resumption of the text of the *Didascalia*.

An old Latin version, on the Verona palimpsest, going back to the end of the fourth century, reproduces three eighths of the work.

Lastly there is a complete translation into Syriac which, like the Latin translation, seems to have followed the composition of the original closely enough.[1]

---

[1] This situation helps to explain why the *Didascalia* is not more widely published and known. Achelis and Flemming (T.U., X, 2, 1904, p. iii) already lamented this state of affairs: "It may seem astonishing that an ecclesiastical Constitution whose great significance for many questions of the New Testament and of the constitution of the Church and her worship is well-known and recognised, should not yet even at this date be accessible to the public in Germany." The situation is no better in France where there is only a single French translation, the first edition of which goes back to 1902. An English translation is mentioned below (p. 202).

### Holy vineyard of his catholic Church

Plantation of God,
Holy vineyard of his catholic Church,

You the chosen who have put your confidence
in the simplicity of the fear of the Lord,

You who have become, through faith,
heirs of his everlasting Kingdom,

You who have received the power and gift of his Spirit,
who have been armed by him,
who have been strengthened in fear,

You who share in the pure and precious blood
poured out by the great God, Jesus Christ,

You who have received the freedom
to call the almighty God Father,
who are co-heirs and friends of his beloved Son,

Listen to the teaching of God,
all you who hope in his promises
and wait (for their fulfilment).                               (ch.1)


### The pardon of sinners

Judge then, O bishop, with authority, as almighty God does;
receive with love those who repent, as almighty God does.
Rebuke, exhort, instruct, for the Lord God has sworn to forgive
all those who have sinned, as he says in Ezekiel:[1]

---

[1] Ezek. 33, 10-11.

And thou, son of man, say to the house of Israel:
You have said:
Our iniquities and our sins weigh upon us
and we rot away beneath them.
How then shall we be able to live?
Proclaim to them: By my life, says the Lord Adonai,
I do not take pleasure in the death of the sinner!
But let the wicked man turn from his way
and live.
Repent therefore,
turn from your evil ways,
and you will not die, house of Israel!

(God), then, here gives hope to those who have sinned that, when they repent, they will find salvation in their repentance. Let them not despair, let them not abide in their sins, let them not increase them! Let them repent, let them lament and weep for their sins, let them be converted with their whole heart (. . .)

(ch. 6)

Teach therefore, O bishop, rebuke, loose (the bonds of sin) with forgiveness. Know that you take the place of almighty God and that you have received the power to forgive sins. For it is to you, bishops, that it was said:

All that you bind upon earth
will be bound in heaven.
And all that you loose
will be loosed (. . .)[1]

When the sinner has undergone repentance and wept, receive

---

[1] See Mt. 18, 18 and 16, 19.

him. And while the people pray for him, lay your hand on him
and allow him once again to dwell in the assembly (. . .)[1]

As a compassionate shepherd, full of love and pity, filled
with care for his flock, watches and counts it, seek out the lost
sheep as the Lord God, Jesus Christ, our good Master and Saviour,
demanded: "Leave the ninety-nine in the mountains, go and look
for the single one that is lost. When you find it, carry it on your
shoulders, rejoice because you have found that which was lost.
Bring it and re-unite it to the flock.[2]

Be obedient then, you too, O bishop, seek out him who has
perished, go and find him who is wandering, bring back him who
has strayed. For you have power to forgive the sins of him who
has fallen since you have put on the person of Christ.

Our Lord also said to him who had sinned:
    "Your sins are forgiven you,
    Your faith has saved you, go in peace."[3]

Now peace means the Church, (the refuge) of serenity and
rest; those whom you deliver from sin, you bring back full of
health and without spot, filled with good hope and ready to
undertake hard and painful tasks. Like a wise and compassionate
physician, heal everyone, above all those who have strayed in
their sins. For "it is not those who are well who need the
physician, but those who are ill".[4]

You too, O bishop, have become a physician in the Church.
Do not cease therefore, with her help, to heal those who are
diseased with sin. Care for them and heal them in every way,

---

[1] Note the community aspect of Christian repentance; sin is an attack on the
holiness of the entire Church; forgiveness too requires the re-integration of the
sinner into the ecclesial community.

[2] See Mt. 18, 10–14 and Lk. 15, 3–7.

[3] See Mt. 9, 2 (= Mk. 2, 5 and Lk. 5, 20), Mk. 5, 32 (= Lk. 8, 48) and Lk. 7, 50.

[4] Mt. 9, 12; Mk. 2, 17; Lk. 5, 31.

restore them to health in the Church. Thus the word of the Lord: "You rule them with violence and cruelty",[1] will not apply to you. You are not then to guide them with violence; do not be hard or curt or pitiless, do not mock the people who are in your hand, do not hide the words of repentance from them.     (ch. 7)

### The prayer of repentance attributed to Manasseh

In the Second Book of Chronicles, the sacred writer relates the history of King Manasseh (687–642), his wickedness, his punishment by deportation to Babylon, his conversion and his return to Jerusalem.[2] The author adds that the prayer which the king made to implore pardon and the restoration of his kingship is to be found in the "Acts of the Kings of Israel" and in the "History of Hozai".[3] We do not possess the text of this prayer. So, towards the beginning of the Christian era, in order to fill in what appeared to be an omission in the inspired text, a hellenistic Jew drew up an apocryphal prayer which he attributed to Manasseh. This pious artifice succeeded completely; many ecclesiastical writers were taken in by it and accepted the "Prayer of Manasseh" as authentic. It had so great a success that many ancient liturgies adopted it as a prayer of repentance.[4]

It is the text of this prayer that the author of the Didascalia has incorporated as a quotation in chapter 7 of his work. Following the traditional structure of Jewish prayers, it is composed of a first part devoted to praise, a second in which forgiveness for sin is implored, and lastly a third which forms the final doxology.

> Almighty Lord, God of our fathers,
> of Abraham, Isaac and Jacob,

---

[1] Ezek. 34, 4.
[2] 2 Chr. 33, 1–20.
[3] 2 Chr. 33, 18, 20.
[4] On the history of this text, see J. B. Frey, art. "Apocryphes de L'Ancien Testament" in *Dict. Bible Supplément*, vol. 1 (1928), col. 442–445 (with bibliography). The text used here is the Greek of the *Apostolic Constitutions*, 2, 22, 12–15; F. X. Funk, *Didascalia et Constitutiones Apostolorum* (Paderborn, 1905), vol. 1, pp. 85–89; P.G. 1, 648A–649A.

and of their just descendants,
thou who didst create the heaven and the earth
with all their splendour,
thou who didst fetter the sea with a word of thy will,
thou who didst close the abyss
and seal it up with thy terrible and glorious name!

The whole universe reveres thee
and trembles before thy power,
for it cannot sustain the magnificence of thy glory,
nor bear the wrath which threatens sinners.
Yet vast and inscrutable
is the mercy that thou hast promised.
For thou art the Lord full of compassion,
patient and rich in mercy,[1]
and thou dost sorrow over the wickedness of men.

For it is thou, Lord,
who, in thy kindness and goodness,
hast promised lenience to repentant sinners.
According to thy mercies
thou dost grant pardon to sinners,
and according to the abundance of thy compassion
thou dost determine the conversion of sinners
for their salvation.

Thou, then, Lord, God of the just,
thou hast not instituted penitence for the just,
for Abraham, Isaac and Jacob;
they did not sin against thee.[2]

---

[1] An allusion to Ex. 34, 6.

[2] The author's reverence for the holiness of the patriarchs is so great that his theology of the universality of sin is somewhat attenuated by it. In fact, all men are

But thou didst institute repentance
for me who am a sinner;
for the number of my sins
is greater than the sand of the sea.

My iniquities are multiplied, Lord,
my iniquities are multiplied;
henceforth I am no longer worthy
to lift my eyes
nor to look towards the depths of heaven.
The number of my evil deeds crushes me
like a long chain of iron.
For I have provoked thine anger,
"that which is wicked in thine eyes, that have I done".[1]

I have committed abominations,[2]
I have multiplied my offences.
And now, in my heart,
I bend my knees before thee.
I beseech thy goodness:
I have sinned, Lord, I have sinned,

---

sinners before God. "Scripture has shut all men up under sin, so that the promise
might be realised through faith in Jesus Christ" (Gal. 3, 22; on this matter see
"Tous enfermés dans le péché" in J. Guillet, *Thèmes Bibliques*, Paris, 1951, pp.
100–116). The author's position seems to have been influenced by certain rabbinic
speculations on the holiness of the patriarchs.

[1] Ps. 51, 6. The Roman liturgy has taken from this text the response *Peccavi
super numerum arenam maris, et multiplicata sunt peccata mea; et non sum dignus videre
altitudinem coeli prae multitudine iniquitatis meae; quoniam irritavi iram tuam, et malum
coram te feci*. It is used particularly, after the third Sunday after Pentecost, every
Sunday, Wednesday and Saturday in July.

[2] Literally: I have raised abominations—the author is here making an implicit
reference to 2 Chr. 33, 2 (this would prove the authenticity of his text), by using
the Greek word *bdelygma*, abomination, which the Septuagint had used in this very
passage. The "abominations" meant idolatrous worship, with the erection of altars
and high places to pagan divinities.

and my iniquities, indeed I know them.[1]
I beg and implore thee:
Forgive me, Lord, forgive me,
do not destroy me with my iniquities,
do not loose against my faults
an eternal anger.[2]
Do not condemn me to the bowels of the earth.

For thou art God,
God of those who turn away from evil.
Show thy goodness toward me
despite my unworthiness,
save me according to thy great mercy.

I will sing thy praises without ceasing
all the days of my life,
for all the powers of heaven
celebrate thee with hymns.
To thee the glory for all ages.
            Amen.


### The great Church, the Bride adorned for God

Hear this, you the laity, the Church chosen by God. The (Jewish) people of old was called "Church", but you you are the catholic Church, holy and perfect, you are a kingly priesthood, a holy community, the people adopted as his inheritance,[3] the great Church, the Bride adorned for God the Lord (. . .)

---

[1] Ps. 51, 5.

[2] The Roman liturgy has utilised this text for the Response *Ne perdideris me cum iniquitatibus meis; neque in finem iratus reserves mala mea.* It is used on Wednesdays between the second and the sixth Sundays after Epiphany.

[3] An allusion to 2 Pet. 2, 9. On the kingly priesthood of the faithful, see L. Cerfaux, "Regale sacerdotium" in *Revue des Sciences Phil. et Théol.*, 28 (1939), pp. 5–39. This article has been reprinted in *Recueil Lucien Cerfaux*, Gembloux, vol. 2, 1954, pp. 283–315.

## The bishop

The high priest is the bishop.[1] He is the servant of the Word and mediator. After God, he teaches you, he is your father who has begotten you by the water (of baptism). He is your leader and guide, the mighty king who leads you to the place of the Almighty.

## The deacon

The deacon holds the place of Christ;[2] you are to love him.

## The deaconess

The deaconess,[3] likewise, is to be honoured by you as the image of the Holy Spirit.

## The priests

Priests are to represent the apostles for you.

---

[1] See J. Colson, "L'évêque dans la Didascalie des apôtres" in *Supp. Vie spirituelle*, 4 (1951), pp. 271–290.

[2] Christian tradition liked to consider Christ as the first "Deacon", whose mission was precisely to serve, *diakonein* (Mt. 20, 28; Mk. 10, 45; Lk. 22, 27). See "Fondements d'une spiritualité du diaconat" in J. Lécuyer, art. "Diaconat" in *Dict. Spir.*, vol. 3 (1957), col. 810–815.

[3] The *Didascalia* often speaks of deaconesses, whose institution seems to go back to the dawn of Christianity (see Rom. 16, 1; 1 Tim. 3, 11 and 5, 9–11). Their ministry was above all an office of prayer and charity. They occupied themselves especially with poor women, with the sick and with pagan women who became catechumens; they assisted and replaced the bishop at the baptism of women, for the rites of immersion and anointing. See J. Daniélou, "Le ministère des femmes dans L'Église primitive" in *La Maison-Dieu*, 61 (1960), pp. 70–96.

## *Widows*

Widows and orphans are to be revered like the altar.[1]

(ch. 9)

### *Good order in the assembly*

At your assemblies in the holy churches, always hold your meetings in an exemplary manner. Arrange the places for the brethren carefully and with all prudence.

## *The place of the bishop and the priests*

For the priests, reserve a place in the eastern part of the house, and set the bishop's throne in the midst of them. The priests are to sit with him.

Laymen are to take their place in the remainder of the eastern side of the house.

It is fitting that the priests be placed in the eastern part of the house with the bishops, then the laymen, then the women. In this way, when you rise to pray, the leaders will be able to rise first, then the laymen and then the women.

You should pray facing the East. For you know that it is written:

> Give thanks to God
> who rides on the heaven of heavens
> on the eastern side.[2]

---

[1] Polycarp had already called widows "the altar of God". (Letter to the Philippians; see *Les Pères Apostoliques*, Vivante Tradition, 1, pp. 77–78).

[2] Ps. 68, 33–34. The quotation here follows the Septuagint translation (reproduced by the Vulgate); the Hebrew actually reads: "Sing to God, sing a

## The place of the deacons

As regards the deacons, let one of them stand continually near the offerings for the Eucharist, and let another stand outside near the door and pay attention to those who enter. Then, when you have made the offerings, let them serve together in the church.

If anyone finds himself in a place other than his own, the deacon who is inside is to take him, make him get up and lead him to the place which belongs to him (. . .)

## The place of the young

Young people are to sit apart, if there is room; if not they are to remain standing.

Those who are older are to sit apart.

## The place of children

Children are to stay at one side, or else their parents are to take them with them and they remain standing.

## The place of women

Again: girls too are to be seated apart; if there is no room, they are to remain standing behind the women.

---

Psalm to him, who rides on the heavens, the ancient heavens." Christian antiquity, as we know, attached great importance to the *orientation* of prayer (the rising sun was regarded as a symbol of Christ, following Zach. 6, 12 and Mal. 4, 2).This orientation of prayer entailed the orientation of churches, which in the East became general in the fifth century and in the West traditional in the sixth. On this subject the following works may be specially consulted: F. J. Dölger, *Sol salutis. Gebet und Gesang im christlichen Altertum mit besonderer Rucksicht auf die Ostung in Gebet und Liturgie*, Münster, 1925: E. Peterson, "La croce e la preghiera verso Oriente" in *Ephem Lit.*, 49 (1945), pp. 52–68.

Married women who are still young and have children are to remain standing apart. Older women and widows are to be seated apart.

## The role of the deacon

The deacon is to watch and see that each person who enters goes to his own place and does not seat himself anywhere else.

Moreover, the deacon is to see that no one drowses or falls asleep, laughs or makes signs. For it is fitting that in the church everyone should maintain an attitude full of dignity and keep wakeful in spirit, so that their ears may be open to the word of the Lord.

## The place of brethren who are passing through

If someone, brother or sister, from another community[1] comes, the deacon is to question them and find out whether they are married, whether she is a faithful widow, whether she is a daughter of the Church or given over to heresy. Then he is to lead them to the place and the seat that is suitable.

## The place of priests and bishops who are passing through

But if a priest from another community comes, you, the priests, are to welcome him into your own place.

And if he is a bishop, he is to sit with the bishop, who is to judge him as worthy as himself and make him share the honour of his place.

---

[1] That is, from another parish.

And you, O bishop, are to ask him if he will be kind enough to speak to your people, for the exhortations and advice of strangers are of great use.

## The place of the poor

If a poor man or a poor woman comes, whether they are from your own parish or from another, above all if they are advanced in years, and if there is no room for them, make a place for them, O bishop, with all your heart, even if you yourself have to sit on the ground.[1]

You must not make any distinction between persons, if you wish your ministry to be pleasing before God.     (ch. 12)

### Fidelity to the meetings of the community

When you are teaching, command and exhort the people to be faithful to the assembly of the church. Let them not fail to attend, but let them gather faithfully together. Let no one deprive the church by staying away; if they do, they deprive the body of Christ of one of its members.

For you must not think only of others, but also of yourselves, when you hear the words which our Lord said: "Who does not gather with me, scatters".[2] Since you are the members of Christ you must not scatter yourselves outside the Church by failing to assemble there. For we have Christ for our Head, as he himself

---

[1] This rule concerning the place of the poor—even if the bishop himself has to sit on the ground!—is inspired by pure gospel tradition, and recalls the text of James 2, 2–4.

[2] Mt. 12, 30; Lk. 11, 23.

promised and announced, in such a way that "you have become sharers with us".[1]

Do not then make light of your own selves, do not deprive our Saviour of his members, do not rend, do not scatter his Body.

(ch. 13)

### Deacons and deaconesses

Bishop, get for yourself workers to care for the poor, helpers who, with you, may lead (the people) to life. Choose those who are pleasing to you before all the people and make them deacons, a man to carry out the numerous tasks that are necessary, and also a woman to look after women.

## Deaconesses

For there are houses where, because of the pagans, you cannot send the deacon to look after the women, but where you could very well send a deaconess.

In many other cases again, the employment of a woman deaconess is necessary. To begin with, when women descend into the water (to receive baptism), it is required that those who descend into the water be anointed by the deaconess with the oil of anointing. Where there is no woman, above all no deaconess,

---

[1] 2 Peter 1, 4. The argument from scripture is weak, the text in fact means: "You have become sharers of the divine nature". But the teaching has a real splendour. It bears witness that the members of the ecclesial community, when they meet together, make up the body of Christ in a special sense and enjoy the presence of the Lord in a privileged manner, according to his promise: "Where two or three are gathered together in my name, I am in the midst of them" (Mt. 18, 20).

it has to be the minister of baptism who himself carries out the anointing of her who is being baptised.[1] But if there is a woman and above all a deaconess, it is not fitting that the women should be seen by men. Give an anointing then only on the head, at the laying on of hands. This is the way in which formerly the kings and priests were anointed in Israel. This is the way in which you, similarly, at the laying on of hands, are to anoint the heads of those who receive baptism, whether they are men or women (. . .)

When the baptised woman comes up out of the water, the deaconess is to receive her and instruct her in purity and holiness, (showing her) that the seal of baptism is unbreakable.

This is the reason for our saying that the service of a woman is required and necessary. For our Lord and Saviour too was served by women deaconesses; these were Mary of Magdala, Mary the mother of James, the mother of Joses, the mother of the sons of Zebedee, as well as other women.[2]      (ch. 16)

---

[1] The *Apostolic Constitutions* omits this phrase. It is easy to understand that the rites of immersion and anointing posed delicate problems when they involved young girls and women. John Moschus (540?-619), in *The Spiritual Meadow*, 3, reports the case of a certain monk, Conon, who had been ordained a priest especially for the administration of baptism, and who found himself acutely troubled by a beautiful young Persian woman, to whom he had to give the rites of anointing. To escape from this embarrassing situation, he resolved to leave his monastery and take refuge in solitude, when John the Baptist appeared to him and strengthened him. Upon which, Conon went on baptising for a further twelve years without ever being troubled again (see R. de Journel, *Jean Moschus, le Pré spirituel*, Sources chrétiennes, 12, Paris, 1946, pp. 48–50).

[2] The *Didascalia* is alluding to the group of women who formed part of the following of Jesus and who assisted (diekonoun) him with their goods (Lk. 8, 2–3). It adds to this group the women listed among the relatives of Jesus (Mt. 13, 55; Mk. 6, 3). The assimilation of these women to deaconesses certainly goes beyond the data of the gospels; but, in the eyes of the author of the *Didascalia*, this reference to Scripture and to the practice of Christ makes an excellent scriptural foundation for the institution of deaconesses.

## Deacons

Deacons are to imitate the bishop in their behaviour. They are to give themselves up completely to their work, not to seek unjust advantages but to be full of enthusiasm for their service.

Their number is to be proportionate to that of the people of the church, so that they can keep everyone in touch and get them help.

To old people who have lost their strength, to brothers and sisters who are afflicted with illness, they are to render willingly the services of which they stand in need.

The woman (deaconess) must be zealous in the service of the women, and the man, the deacon, in the service of men. He is to be ready to obey the orders of the bishop. Everywhere that he is sent to be of service and to carry a message, he is to be active and painstaking. For each must know his duty and apply himself to fulfilling it.

Be too of one will, one spirit, one soul, even if you are two in body. Recognise what the diaconate is, as our Lord and Saviour has defined it in the Gospel:

> He from among you
> who wishes to be your master,
> let him be your servant.
> Thus the Son of man
> did not come to be ministered to
> but to minister
> and to give his life
> in ransom for many.[1]

(ch. 16)

---

[1] Mt. 20, 26, 28.

### Doxology

To him who has power and might
to open the ears of your heart,
so that you may receive
the penetrating[1] words of the Lord
in the Gospel and in the teaching
of Jesus Christ of Nazareth,

To him who, in the days of Pontius Pilate,
was crucified and who died
to proclaim to Abraham, Isaac and Jacob
the end of the world
and the coming resurrection of the dead,

To him who rose from the dead
to proclaim to you
and to give you to know
that he is the pledge of the Resurrection,

To him who ascended to the heavens
by the power of God, his Father,
and of the Holy Spirit,

To him who sits to the right
on the throne of the All-mighty,
above the Cherubim,

---

[1] Or "sharp" (Achelis-Flemming, *Die syrische Didaskalia*, T.U., X, 2, 1904, p. 145, translate as: "die scharfe Worte"). The text recalls Heb. 4, 12: "The Word of God is living, effective and sharper than any two-edged sword, it penetrates to the very division of soul and spirit."

To him who is to come
with power and with glory
to judge the dead and the living:

To him be dominion and honour, majesty and kingship
as to the Father and to the Holy Spirit,
to (God) "who is, who was and who is to be"[1]
now and from age to age
and in all eternity.
                    Amen.

---

[1] A stereotyped formula borrowed from the doxologies of the Apocalypse
(1, 4, 8; 4, 8; 11, 17). It takes its inspiration from the divine name "I am he who
is" (Ex. 3, 14) and emphasises the eternity of God.

# 6

# The Euchology of Serapion of Thmuis

*(about 350)*

# Serapion, Bishop of Thmuis († after 362)

## The man

We possess only very fragmentary information about the life of Serapion.

We know that he had retired to the desert where he had become one of the favourite disciples of St Anthony (250–356). Some time before 339 he became Bishop of Thmuis, a small region in Lower Egypt. He seems to have taken part in the Council of Sardica in 343 and at it to have supported the cause of St Athanasius of Alexandria (295–373). About 356 the latter sent him, with four other bishops and three priests, on an embassy to the emperor Constantius, to refute the accusations which the Arians had brought against him. Athanasius addressed several letters to him, of which one is on the death of Arius,[1] and some theological writings on the Holy Spirit.[2]

We do not know the year in which Serapion died. But since the correspondence of Athanasius dates from the years 356–362, his death must have taken place after 362.

## The work

According to St Jerome, Serapion united to great holiness of life a brilliant intelligence which won him the surname *scholasticus*, the Scholar.[3] All of his, however, that tradition has preserved is two letters, a polemical work *Against the Manichaeans*—mentioned by St Jerome, partially reconstituted in 1894 by Brinkmann and edited in its entirety in 1931—and a *Euchology*.[4]

It is this last work, discovered in 1894 at Mount Athos, which

---

[1] *P.G.* 25, 685–690.

[2] *P.G.* 26, 529–676.

[3] *De Viris Illustribus*, 99; see G. Bardy, art. "Serapion" in *D.T.C.*, vol. 14, col. 1908–1912.

[4] For a bibliography of the works of Serapion, see especially Altaner-Chirat, *Précis de Patrologie*, 1961, p. 401.

has especially drawn the attention of theologians and liturgists today. It is a kind of Ritual containing thirty liturgical prayers. The first twelve were used in the first part of the Sunday synaxis,[1] centred on readings and prayer.[2] There follow the anaphora, which is the most precious document of the whole collection,[3] the prayers of the liturgies of baptism[4] and confirmation,[5] a prayer over the oil of the sick and another for the dead.[6]

Without doubt Serapion has left his own mark on more than one of these texts before transcribing it into his *Euchology*; textual analysis and comparison with other formularies enable us to discover some of the points at which they have been retouched. But the fact that these prayers were meant in some way to represent the official liturgy at Thmuis in the mid fourth century and that some of them certainly date from well before that epoch, can only heighten the value of the witness to the faith of the Church which they provide.

## *The Sunday Synaxis*

## *1. First Prayer for Sunday*

> We pray thee, Father of the only-begotten Son,
> Lord of all things,
> Creator of the created world,
> Author of what exists.
>
> Our pure hands
> we hold out towards thee;
> and our spirits
> we raise towards thee,

---

[1] These prayers are given here in the order adopted by F. X. Funk, *Didascalia et constitutiones apostolorum*, Paderborn, 1905, vol. 2, see pp. 158–194.

[2] See pp. 100–113.

[3] See pp. 113–118.

[4] See pp. 122–127.

[5] See pp. 128f.

[6] See pp. 131–134.

We pray thy mercy,
thy pity and thy goodness;
amend us, increase in us
power, faith and knowledge.


Cast thine eyes on us, Lord,
we lay our weaknesses before thee.
Grant pardon and mercy to us all.
Have pity on thy people,
show them thy goodness,
make them generous, chaste and pure.


Send the angelic spirits
that thine entire people
may be holy and unspotted.


We pray thee,
send thy Holy Spirit into our souls.
Grant us to understand
the Scriptures which he inspired,
to interpret them clearly and worthily,
so that all the people here present
may draw profit from them,


Through thine only-begotten Son, Jesus Christ,
in the Holy Spirit.
Through him, glory to thee and power,
  now and for ever and ever.
          Amen.

## 2. *Prayer after the sermon*

Saviour God, God of the universe,
Sovereign and Creator of all things,
Father of the only-begotten Son,
the living and true Image born of thee:[1]
thou hast sent him for the good of the human race;
through him thou hast called all men
and thou hast reconciled them.

We pray thee for this people:
Send them the Holy Spirit,
that the Lord Jesus may come to visit them,
that he may speak in the spirit of each,
that he may prepare their hearts for faith,
that he may lead their souls to thee,
O God of mercy.
Take possession too
of thy people in this town,
take possession of thy noble flock,
Through thine only-begotten Son, Jesus Christ,
in the Holy Spirit.
Through him, glory to thee and power,
now and for ever and ever.
     Amen.

## 3. *Prayer for the catechumens*

Lord of the universe (thou our) help,
deliverer of the delivered,
Master of those who are saved,
hope of those who are in thy hand!

---

[1] Heb. 1, 3.

It is thou who hast taken away iniquity,
who, through thine only Son, hast destroyed Satan,
put an end to his undertakings
and delivered those whom he had enchained.

We give thee thanks for the catechumens,
whom thou hast called through thine only Son,
to whom thou hast given to know thee.

For this reason we beg thee
to strengthen them in this knowledge,
so "that they may know thee,
thee the one true God,
and him whom thou hast sent, Jesus Christ".[1]

Keep them in thy teachings
and in thy pure doctrine;
let them make progress in it,
let them become worthy of the "bath of regeneration"[2]
and of thy holy mysteries,

Through thine only-begotten Son, Jesus Christ,
in the Holy Spirit,
now and for ever and ever.
    Amen.


## 4. *Blessing of the catechumens*

To thee, Master, we lift our hands
and pray thee
to stretch out thine own divine and life-giving hand
to bless this people.

---

[1] John 17, 3.
[2] Tit. 3, 5.

Before thee, eternal Father,[1] through thine only Son,
see, they have bowed their heads.

Let thy blessing descend on this people,
the blessing of knowledge and of piety,
the blessing of thy holy mysteries,

Through thine only-begotten Son, Jesus Christ.
Through him, glory to thee and power,
in the Holy Spirit,
now and for ever and ever.
      Amen.

## 5. *Litany for the people*

We bless thee, O God who lovest mankind,
we set before thee our weakness,
we pray thee to be our strength.

Pardon our past sins,
forgive us our former faults,
make of us new men,
make of us servants pure and generous.[2]

We consecrate ourselves to thee.
Accept us, O God of truth,

---

[1] Serapion frequently gives to the Father the title *agenetos* (*Euchology* 4, 5, 12, 13, 17, 19, 27) which means literally "that which has not had birth, or beginning" and which is translated here by "eternal". The *Apostolic Constitutions* (VII, 41, 4; VIII, 6, 9, and 11; VIII, 14, 3; pp. 155, 163, 180) prefer the titles *agennetos*, literally "not begotten, not created", which is translated by "uncreated".

[2] *Generous* and *true* translate the same word *gnesios* which means "of (good) birth", "legitimate" (Titus and Timothy are *true* sons in the faith, Tit. 1, 4; 1 Tim. 1, 2) whence the meaning "noble", "generous" (in the old sense of "of noble descent"). The *gnesios* people represents the authentic people of God.

accept this people,
that it may be wholly (thy) true (people).[1]

Make them live wholly in innocence and uprightness.
Let them be joined to the heavenly spirits,
let them be counted among the angels,
let them all be chosen and holy.

We pray to thee for those who believe and acknowledge the Lord Jesus Christ. May they be strengthened in faith,[2] in knowledge and in doctrine.

We pray to thee for all this people. Pardon them all, show thyself, reveal thy light; that all may acknowledge thee, eternal Father, together with thine only-begotten Son, Jesus Christ.

We pray to thee for all magistrates. May their government be peaceful, for the tranquillity of the Church.

We pray to thee, God of mercies, for free men and for slaves, for men and women, for the poor and the rich. Show thy goodwill to all; extend thy goodness to us; have pity on all; guide their steps towards thyself; give to all the grace of conversion.

We pray to thee for travellers. Give them the angel of peace to accompany them; let no harm befall them, let them come to their harbour and their destination in great security.

We pray to thee for the afflicted, the captives and the poor. Strengthen them all, save them from their bonds, deliver

---

[1] See note 2 on opposite page.
[2] An allusion to Col. 2, 7.

them from their wretchedness, console them all, thou who art consolation and strength.

We pray to thee for the sick. Give them health, relieve their sickness, grant to them perfect health of body and soul.

Thou art Saviour and Benefactor,
thou art Lord and King of all!

To thee we make our prayer for all
through thine only-begotten Son, Jesus Christ.

Through him, glory to thee and power,
in the Holy Spirit,
now and for ever and ever.
    Amen.

## 6. *Blessing of the people*

May the pure and living hand,
the hand of the only-begotten Son,
the hand which removes all evils,
which strengthens and fortifies all that is holy,
be stretched out over the bowed heads of this people!

May this people be blessed
with the blessing of the Spirit,
with the blessing of heaven,
with the blessing of the prophets and the apostles.

May the bodies of all be blessed
for purity and chastity;
may their souls be blessed
for understanding, knowledge and the mysteries.

May all together be blessed
through thine only-begotten Son, Jesus Christ.
Through him, glory to thee and power,
in the Holy Spirit,
now and for ever and ever.
 Amen.


## 7. *Prayer for the sick*

We pray thee, Guardian and Lord,
Maker of the body and creator of the soul,
thou who dost fashion man,
who dost administer and govern,
who dost save the whole human race,
who dost reconcile and bring peace
because of thy love for mankind!

Be favourable, Lord,
succour and heal all the sick,
control their maladies,
relieve those who languish.
"Give glory to thy holy name",[1]
through thine only-begotten Son, Jesus Christ.

Through him, glory to thee and power,
in the Holy Spirit,
now and for ever and ever.
 Amen.

---

[1] Ps. 115, 1.

## 8. *Blessing of the sick*

Lord, God of mercies,
deign to stretch out thine hands,
in thy kindness, heal all the sick,
in thy kindness, make them worthy of health,
deliver them from their present sickness;
in the name of thine only-begotten Son, grant them recovery;
let this holy name be the remedy
for health and restoration.
Through him, glory to thee and power,
in the Holy Spirit,
now and for ever and ever.
Amen.

## 9. *Prayer for the harvest*

Creator of heaven and earth,
who dost adorn the heaven with the choir of stars
and illuminate it with sparkling points of light,
who dost load the earth with fruits
for the use of men:
in thy kindness, thou dost give
to the human race thou didst create
to rejoice in the brilliance and clearness of the stars
and to be nourished on the fruits of the earth.

We pray thee, give us
most abundant and fertilising rains;
grant also that the earth may produce fruits
in great plenty,
because of thy love for mankind
and because of thy good-will.

Be mindful of those who call on thee.
Honour thy one, holy, catholic Church,
hear our prayers and supplications,
and bless the whole earth
through thine only-begotten Son, Jesus Christ.

Through him, glory to thee and power,
in the Holy Spirit,
now and for ever and ever.
    Amen.


## 10. *Prayer for the Church*

Lord, God of ages,
God of the heavenly spirits,[1]
God of pure souls
and of all those who call on thee
in all sincerity and purity,
thou who, in heaven, dost manifest thyself
and make thyself known to the pure spirits,
thou to whom, on earth, hymns are sung,
and who dost dwell in the catholic Church,
thou whom the holy angels and pure souls serve,
thou who didst make of heaven a living choir
to glorify and praise the truth!

Make this Church to be living and pure,
grant her to possess divine powers,
to have at her service the pure angels
so that she may be able to celebrate thee purely.

---

[1] Literally: "endowed with reason".

We pray thee for all the men of this Church.
To all, grant thy favour,
to all, reconciliation,
to all, pardon of their sins.
Grant them to sin no more henceforth.
Be thou a rampart for them
and destroy all temptation.

Have pity on men, women and children.
Manifest thyself to all,
that knowledge of thee "may be graven on their hearts".[1]

Through thine only-begotten Son, Jesus Christ.
Through him, glory to thee and power,
in the Holy Spirit,
now and for ever and ever.
    Amen.


## *11. Litany for the clergy and people*

We call on thee, Saviour and Lord, God of all flesh, and Lord of
    every spirit, thou who art blessed and dost dispense all
    blessing.

Make holy our bishop, preserve him from all temptation, give
    him wisdom and knowledge, grant him to make progress
    in the knowledge of thee.

We pray thee too for those who are priests with him. Make them
    holy, give them wisdom, knowledge and right doctrine,

---

[1] An allusion to the "New Covenant" (Jer. 31, 33; Heb. 8, 10) in which God
is going to engrave his Law on the hearts of the faithful.

grant them to dispense thy holy teachings rightly and without reproach.

Make the deacons holy too. Let them be pure in heart and body, let them be able to fulfil their ministry with a pure conscience, to present the sacred body and blood (of the Lord).

We entreat thee too for the subdeacons, the readers and the interpreters.[1] Be strength and consolation for all the ministers of the Church; to all of them bring pity, mercy and spiritual growth.

We pray thee for hermits and those who live in virginity. Let them finish their race undefiled, their life with perseverance; let them be able to pass all their days in purity and holiness.

Have pity also on all those who are married, men, women and children. Give thy blessing to all so that they may progress and be improved, so that they may be found among the living and elect.

Through thine only-begotten Son, Jesus Christ.
Through him, glory to thee and power,
in the Holy Spirit,
now and for ever and ever.
    Amen.

## 12. *Prayer at the genuflection*

Father of the only-begotten Son,
full of goodness and mercy,
thou who dost love men and dost love souls,
Benefactor of all those who turn to thee.

---

[1] I.e., those who translated the readings and sermons for the benefit of the faithful who would not have heard them in their usual tongue.

Hear our entreaty,
grant us knowledge and faith,
piety and holiness.

Curb all passion and all sensuality,
every fault of thy people,
grant them all to become pure,
reconcile and pardon all their offences.

For it is before thee, O eternal Father,
through thine only-begotten Son,
that we bend the knee.
Give us a holy spirit, a perfect help,
give us to seek thee and to love thee,
to examine and search out thy divine words.

Give us thy hand, O master,
and lift us up.
Raise us, O God of mercies!
Let our regard be lifted towards thee,
let our eyes be opened!

In thy kindness, give us confidence,
do not allow us to be put to the blush,
to be covered with confusion,
or to have to pass judgment on ourselves.

Cancel the decree which is against us,[1]
write our names in "the book of life",[2]
count us among thy holy prophets
and among thine apostles,

---

[1] An allusion to Col. 2, 14. God has cancelled "the bond (of our debt) which was against us . . . he has set it aside, nailing it to the Cross", thus manifesting the reality of the pardon he has granted us through the sacrifice of Christ.

[2] Phil. 4, 3; Apoc. 13, 8.

Through thine only-begotten Son, Jesus Christ.
Through him, glory to thee and power,
in the Holy Spirit,
now and for ever and ever.
Amen.

### The Eucharistic Liturgy

### 13. Prayer of the Anaphora[1]

## Preface

It is worthy and just to praise thee,
to celebrate thee, to glorify thee,
eternal Father of the only-begotten Son, Jesus Christ.

We praise thee, eternal God,
inscrutable, indescribable,
incomprehensible to every created nature.

We praise thee, thou who art known to the only Son,
thou whom he reveals, whom he unfolds,
whom he makes known to created nature.

We praise thee, thou who knowest the Son
and dost reveal his glory to the holy,
thou who art known to the Son whom thou hast begotten,
thou whom he manifests and unfolds to the holy.

---

[1]See B. Capelle, "L'Anaphore de Sérapion, Essai d'exégèse" in *Le Muséon*, 59, 1–4 (1946), pp. 425–443.

We praise thee, invisible Father
who givest immortality.
Thou art the source of life, the source of light,
the source of all grace and all truth.
Thou lovest men, thou lovest the poor,
thou dost reconcile thyself with all,
thou drawest all to thee
through the coming of thy beloved Son.

We pray thee, make of us living men.
Give us the Spirit of light
"that we may know thee, thee the True
and him whom thou hast sent, Jesus Christ".[1]

Give us the Holy Spirit that we may be able
to proclaim and tell forth indescribable mysteries!
May the Lord Jesus speak in us
and also the Holy Spirit.
May he celebrate thee with hymns through us!

For thou art above every Principality,
Power, Force and Domination,
above every name that is named
in this age as in the age to come.

## Sanctus

Thou art attended by thousands upon thousands
and myriads upon myriads
of Angels and Archangels,
of Thrones and Dominions,
of Principalities and Powers.

---

[1] John 17, 3.

Beside thee stand
the two august Seraphim with six wings:
two to cover their face,
two to cover their feet,
two with which to fly.
They sing thy holiness.
With theirs, accept also
our acclamations of thy holiness:
Holy, holy, holy is the Lord Sabaoth!
Heaven and earth are filled with thy glory.[1]
The heaven is filled, the earth is filled
with thy wonderful glory!

## *The account of the Institution*

Lord[2] of Powers, fill this sacrifice too
with thy power and thy participation.
It is to thee that we have offered[3]
this living sacrifice, this bloodless offering.
It is to thee that we have offered this bread,
figure of the body of thine only-begotten Son.
The bread is the figure of the holy body.

---

[1] See Is. 6, 2–3.

[2] This paragraph (*Lord of Powers . . . holy body*) is without doubt an addition to the primitive text. It is dogmatic in character but composed on an ancient model; the expression *figure of the body* is an archaism which is found again in the anaphora of St Ambrose: "This offering . . . which is the figure of the body and of the blood of our Lord Jesus Christ, *quod est figura corporis et sanguinis Domini nostri Jesus Christi*" (*De Sacramentis*, IV, 5, 21; see B. Botte, *Ambroise de Milan, Des sacrements. Des mystères*, Sources chrétiennes, 256, Paris, 1961, p. 114).

[3] The perfect tense of *we have offered* seems to be an intentional modification; Serapion has altered the source which he was using to recall the action at the offertory when the offerings are put on the altar.

For the Lord Jesus, the night when he was betrayed,
took bread, broke it
and gave it to his disciples saying:
"Take and eat, this is my body,
which is broken for you
for the remission of sins."

For this reason,[1] we too,
celebrating the memorial of his death,
have offered this bread and pray:
through this sacrifice, reconcile us all to thyself,
be favourable to us, O God of truth.
For just as this bread,
once scattered upon the hills,
has been joined together to become but one,
so too, deign to reunite thy holy Church
from every people, from every land,
from every town, village and house,
and make her one single Church,
living and catholic.

We offer too the cup, figure of the blood.
For the Lord Jesus, after the meal,
took the cup and said to his disciples:
"Take and drink,
this is the New Testament,
that is, my blood poured out for you
for the remission of sins."
For this reason we too have offered
the cup, figure of the blood.

---

[1] Serapion has boldly introduced into the primitive thread of the narrative of the Institution a little anamnesis and a borrowing from the *Didache* (the paragraph *For this reason . . . living and catholic*; for the *Didache* see p. 14). This insertion is a prayer for the unity of the Church from which the Arian heresy had snatched so many of the faithful "of every country, town, village and house".

## Invocation of the Word[1]

O God of truth,
may thy holy Word come down upon this bread,
that it may become the body of the Word,
and upon this cup,
that it may become the blood of the Truth.
Grant that all who communicate
may receive a life-giving remedy,
which may heal every infirmity in them,
which may strengthen them for all progress and all virtue,
let it not be a cause, O God of truth,
of condemnation, confusion or shame.

## Memento of the living

For we call on thee, O eternal (God),
through thine only Son, in the Holy Spirit:
Take pity on this people,
judge them worthy of progress.
Send thine Angels to this people,
to help them to triumph over the Evil One
and strengthen thy Church.

---

[1] It is very surprising to read here, in place of the traditional epiclesis addressed to the Holy Spirit, an invocation of the Word. This anomaly originates "in the innovating spirit of the bishop of Thmuis" (B. Capelle, op. cit., p. 443), who is fond of emphasising the sanctifying action of the incarnate Word. There is a suggestion here of the friend of St Athanasius and of the polemic against the Arians. (We know that the fathers of the Church often used the sanctifying work of the Holy Spirit as a starting point for proving his divinity. See for example St Basil's *Treatise on the Holy Spirit*. Serapion uses the same line of argument to affirm the divinity of the Word.) Other prayers asking for the descent of the Word are to be found in the *Euchology* (19, 22, 25, 29), although these prayers were used traditionally of the Holy Spirit.

## Memento of the dead

> We pray thee too for all the dead
> who have fallen asleep,
> whom we call to mind.

After recalling the names:

> Sanctify these souls,
> for thou knowest them all.
> Sanctify those who have fallen asleep in the Lord.
> Number them with thy holy Powers
> give them a place and a dwelling in thy Kingdom.

## Final prayer and doxology

> Accept the thanksgiving of thy people.
> Bless those who have presented to thee
> these offerings and thanksgivings.
> Give all this people health,
> prosperity and happiness,
> all good things of soul and body.

> Through thine only-begotten Son, Jesus Christ,
> in the Holy Spirit,
> as he was, as he is and will be,
> from generation to generation
> and for ever and ever.
>       Amen.

## *14. Prayer at the breaking of the bread*

Make us worthy too to participate in thee,[1]
O God of truth,
and grant that our bodies may progress in purity,
our souls in understanding and knowledge.
Give us wisdom, O God of mercies,
through receiving the body and the blood (of Christ).

Glory to thee and power,
through the only-begotten Son,
in the Holy Spirit,
now and for ever and ever.
  Amen.

## *15. Blessing of the people after the breaking of the bread*

I lift my hand over this people
and I pray thee to stretch out the hand of truth
and to bless this people here
in the name of thy love for men,
O God of mercies,
and in the name of the mysteries which we celebrate.

Let the hand of love and power,
the hand of wisdom, purity and all holiness
bless this people and keep them
so that they may progress and be improved,

---

[1] "To participate in thee", literally "of thy participation". The word participation, *koinonia*, is the technical term for participation in God (I Cor. 1, 9: "You have been called to participation in his Son"); it also means "communion" which is participation in the body and blood of Christ (I Cor. 10, 16: "Participation in the blood . . . in the body").

Through thine only-begotten Son, Jesus Christ,
in the Holy Spirit,
now and for ever and ever.
    Amen.


## 16. *Prayer after the communion of the people*

We give thee thanks, O Master,
for having called those who were in error,
for having reconciled those who had sinned.
Thou hast passed over the threat which weighed on us,
through thy love for men, thou hast withdrawn it,
through conversion, thou hast abandoned it,
through thy knowledge, thou hast rejected it.

We give thee thanks
for having made us to "participate in the body and the blood".[1]
Bless us and bless this people.
Grant us to have a share in the body and the blood.

Through thine only-begotten Son.
Through him, glory to thee and power,
in the Holy Spirit,
now and for ever and ever.
    Amen.


## 17. *Blessing of oil and water*

In the name of thine only Son, Jesus Christ,
we bless these creatures.[2]

---

[1] I Cor. 10, 19.
[2] For the significance of these blessings see p. 41.

We invoke the name of him who suffered,
who was crucified, who rose from the dead
and sits at the right hand of the Eternal,
on this water and on this oil.
Give these creatures the power to heal,
let them drive out every fever,
every demon and every sickness.
Let them become for those who use them[1]
a healing and reviving remedy,
in the name of the only-begotten Son, Jesus Christ.

Through him, glory to thee and power,
in the Holy Spirit,
now and for ever and ever.
    Amen.


## 18. *Laying on of hands after the blessing of oil and water*

God of truth who dost love men,
keep thy people in the participation
in the body and the blood.

Let their bodies be living bodies,
their souls be pure souls.

Grant thy blessing to keep them
in the participation (in the body and blood),

To procure security for them
thanks to the Eucharist we have celebrated.[2]

---

[1] "For those who use them", literally: "Through the fact of drinking (this water) and through anointing".

[2] The translation here is uncertain; literally: in the "stability" (or "security") of the accomplished Eucharist.

Make them blessed, all of them together,
and set them among thine elect,

Through thine only-begotten Son, Jesus Christ,
in the Holy Spirit,
now and for ever and ever.
    Amen.


*The Liturgy of Baptism, Confirmation and Holy Orders*

## 19. *Consecration of the baptismal waters*

King and Lord of all things,
Creator of the universe:
Through the Incarnation[1] of thine only Son, Jesus Christ,
thou hast given to all created nature the grace of salvation;
thou hast redeemed thy creation
by the coming of thine unutterable Word.
Look down now from the height of heaven,
cast thine eyes[2] on these waters,
fill them with the Holy Spirit.

Let thine unutterable Word be in them,
let him transform their power.
Let him give them the power to be fertile,
let him fill them with thy grace,
so that the mystery which is to be accomplished
may bear fruit in those who are going to be regenerated
and may fill with thy divine grace
all those who go down (into the baptismal fount)
and are baptised.

---

[1] Literally: the "descent" (*katabasis*).
[2] An allusion to Ps. 80, 15.

Thou who dost love men, be gracious,
take pity on those thou didst create,
save thy creation, the work of thy right hand.
Transfigure all those who are going to be re-born
with thy divine and unspeakable beauty.
Transfigured and regenerated,
let them thus be saved,
"be judged worthy of thy Kingdom".[1]

Just as the Word, thine only-begotten Son,
by descending into the waters of the Jordan,
conferred sanctification on them,
even so let him descend now into these waters
to render them holy and spiritual,
so that the baptised
may no longer be "flesh and blood",[2]
but may become "spiritual".
Let them be able to adore thee, the eternal Father,
through Jesus Christ, in the Holy Spirit.

Through him, glory to thee and power
for ever and ever.
            Amen.


## 20. *Prayer of exorcism*

We pray thee, O God of truth,
for thy servant who is here.

---

[1] 2 Thess. 1, 5.

[2] See Jn. 3, 6: "That which is born of the flesh is flesh, that which is born of the Spirit is spirit." Relying on this text, Didymus remarks: "The man who has not received baptism is fleshly, that is to say, he does not yet participate in the divine light. . . . But he who has been baptised is 'spiritual', that is to say, he participates in immortal life" (*On the Trinity*, bk. 2, ch. 12; *P.G.* 39, 673A).

We beg thee to make him worthy
of the divine mystery and of thine unutterable regeneration,

For it is to thee who lovest men
that we offer him,
It is to thee that we consecrate him.

According to thy grace, let him share in this regeneration,
let him no longer be under the influence
of any gloomy and wicked spirit;
but let him serve thee at all times,
let him keep thy commandments,
let the Word, thine only-begotten Son, guide him.

Through him glory to thee and power,
in the Holy Spirit,
now and for ever and ever.
      Amen.


## 21. *Prayer after the renunciation*

Almighty Lord, seal with thine approval
the assent which thy servant here
has now given thee.[1]

Keep firm his moral life and his conduct.
Let him no longer henceforth be the slave of evil,
but serve the God of truth.

Let him submit himself, to the very end,
to thee, the Creator of the universe,
and show himself a true (son).[2]

---

[1] Compare with this the ritual given in the *Apostolic Tradition* of Hippolytus, "The Renunciation of Satan", p. 58.

[2] I.e., a legitimate son, *gnesios*; see p. 104. n. 2.

Through thine only-begotten Son, Jesus Christ.
Through him glory to thee and power,
in the Holy Spirit,
now and for ever and ever.
 Amen.

## 22. *Prayer for the anointing of the catechumens*[1]

O Master, thou who lovest men
and who lovest souls,
God of mercy, pity and truth,[2]
we call on thee for those
who come to follow thee,[3]
and we entrust them to the promises of thine only Son
who said, "Those whose sins you shall forgive,
they shall be forgiven them."[4]

We anoint with this oil these men and women
who present themselves for this divine regeneration.

We beseech our Lord Jesus Christ
to give them the power which heals and strengthens.

Let him manifest himself through this anointing,
let him remove from their souls,
from their bodies or their spirits,
every sign of sin, of iniquity
or of the work of the devil.

---

[1] See the anointing at the exorcism in the *Apostolic Tradition*, p. 58.
[2] A phrase borrowed from Ps. 86, 15.
[3] I.e., who become disciples of Christ.
[4] John 20, 23.

Let him, through his own grace,
grant them forgiveness.
Freed from sin,
let them live for righteousness.[1]

Now that they have become a new creation through this
    anointing,
purified by this bath and renewed by the Spirit,[2]
let them have the power to overcome henceforth
all the forces of the enemy
which are ranged against them,
and all the deceits of this life.
Let them be gathered and re-united to the flock
of the Lord and of our Saviour Jesus Christ.
Let them share with the saints
the promised inheritance.

Through him, glory to thee and power,
in the Holy Spirit,
for ever and ever.
        Amen.

## 23. *Prayer after the anointing*

Thou who lovest men, Benefactor,
Saviour of all who turn to thee:

Be gracious to this servant here;
let thy right hand lead him to regeneration.

---

[1] Cf. Rom. 6, 18: "Freed from sin, you have become slaves to righteousness."
Baptism delivers the neophytes from slavery to sin, but introduces them into a new
"service", that of righteousness, a service which bears fruit in holiness and opens
on to eternal life (Rom. 6, 22).

[2] An allusion to Titus 3, 5.

Let thine only-begotten Son, the Word,
draw him to the (baptismal) fount.

Let his new birth be honoured,
let thy grace not be fruitless.

Let thy holy Word be beside him,
let thy Holy Spirit be with him,
let him repel and put to flight every temptation,

Through thine only-begotten Son, Jesus Christ,
glory to thee and power,
now and for ever and ever.
　　Amen.


*After baptism*

## 24. *Prayer for the neophytes*

God, O God of truth, Creator of the universe
and Lord of all creation,
richly endow thy servant here with thy blessing.
Make him to share in the angelic powers,
so that henceforth he, who has had a part
in thy divine and profitable grace,
may be no longer "flesh" but "spirit".[1]
Keep him, to the very end, for thyself,
O Creator of all things,

Through thine only-begotten Son, Jesus Christ.
Through him, glory to thee and power,
in the Holy Spirit,
now and for ever and ever.
　　Amen.

---

[1] See John 3, 6; p. 123, n. 2.

*Confirmation*

## 25. *Prayer for the confirmed*[1]

God of the (heavenly) powers.
Help of every soul who turns to thee
and who places himself under the powerful hand
of thine only-begotten Son, we call on thee:
By the divine and invisible power
of the Lord and our Saviour Jesus Christ,
carry out through this oil thy divine and heavenly work.

Those who have been baptised receive the anointing,
(they are marked) with the impress of the sign
of the saving Cross of the only-begotten Son.
By this Cross Satan and every hostile power
have been defeated and are led captive[2]
in the triumphal procession.

Regenerated and renewed
by the bath of new birth,
let these here also share
in the gifts of the Holy Spirit.

Strengthened by the seal,
let them remain "steadfast and immovable",[3]
sheltered from all attack and pillaging,
subjected neither to insult nor aggression.

---

[1] This prayer is given the title: "Prayer over the oil of the post-baptismal anointings". It means certainly the post-baptismal anointing which accompanied the rite of confirmation (see p. 60, n. 2). The neophyte is placed "under the powerful hand of the only-begotten Son", i.e., has received the laying on of hands, and has been marked with the "impress of the sign of the saving cross".

[2] The verb *ethriambeuthe* means, in the active sense, "to triumph over someone", hence "to lead (captive) in the triumphal procession". The text alludes to Col. 2, 15: "(Christ) having disarmed the principalities and powers, has made a public spectacle of them, having led them in his triumph (*thriambeusas*)."

[3] I Cor. 15, 58.

Let them live to the very end
in the faith and knowledge of the truth,[1]
in the expectation of the hope of heavenly life
and of the eternal promises
of the Lord and our Saviour, Jesus Christ.

Through him, glory to thee and power,
in the Holy Spirit,
now and for ever and ever.
Amen.

*Ordination prayers*

## 26. *The laying on of hands for the ordination of deacons*

Father of the only-begotten Son, who hast sent thy Son, who hast arranged the things of the earth in wisdom,

who hast given rules and orders to thy Church for the profit and the salvation of the flock,

who hast chosen bishops, priests and deacons to serve thy catholic Church,

who through thine only-begotten Son didst choose seven deacons and according to thy grace didst give them the Holy Spirit:[2]

Appoint thy servant here also to be a deacon of thy catholic Church.

Give him the Spirit of knowledge and of discernment so that

---

[1] A borrowing from II Thess. 2, 13 and I Tim. 2, 4.
[2] See the institution of deacons in Acts 6, 1-6.

he may be able, in the midst of thy holy people, to serve this
ministry in a pure and untarnished manner.[1]

> Through thine only-begotten Son, Jesus Christ,
> in the Holy Spirit,
> now and for ever and ever.
>     Amen.

## 27. *The laying on of hands for the ordination of priests*

We raise our hands, O Master, God of heaven, Father of
thine only-begotten Son, over this man and pray thee:

That the Spirit of truth may dwell in him.

According to thy grace, grant him understanding, knowledge
and a good heart.

Let the divine Spirit be with him so that he may be able to
administer thy people, to be the ambassador of thy divine words,
to reconcile the people to thee, O eternal God.

According to thy grace, through the Spirit of Moses thou
hast poured out the Spirit of holiness upon the elect: grant also
to this (man), through the Spirit of thine only-begotten Son, the
Holy Spirit in graces of wisdom, knowledge and right faith, so
that he may be able to serve thee with a pure conscience.

> Through thine only-begotten Son, Jesus Christ.
> Through him, glory to thee and power,
> in the Holy Spirit,
> now and for ever and ever.
>     Amen.

---

[1] The text plays on the double meaning of the word *diakonein*, "to serve" and
"to be a deacon".

## 28. *The laying on of hands for the consecration of a bishop*

Thou who didst send the Lord Jesus to buy back the whole world,

thou who, through him, didst choose the apostles and from age to age hast ordained holy bishops, O God of truth:

Make of (thy servant) here a living bishop, a holy bishop in the succession of the apostles.

Give him the grace of the divine Spirit that thou hast granted to all the true servants, to the prophets and the patriarchs.

Render him worthy to feed thy flock, let him abide in the episcopate without reproach or fault.

> Through thine only-begotten Son, Jesus Christ.
> Through him, glory to thee and power,
> in the Holy Spirit,
> now and for ever and ever.
> Amen.

*Prayers for the sick and for the dead*

## 29. *Prayer over the oil of the sick, over the bread and the water*

We call on thee,
thou who dost control every authority and power,
thou, "the Saviour of all men",[1]
the Father of our Lord and Saviour Jesus Christ.

---

[1] I Tim. 4, 10.

We beg thee to send,
from the height of heaven (where thine) only-begotten Son
   (reigns),
a power of healing into this oil.
For those who receive anointing
or make use of these creatures,
let it put to flight "every disease and every infirmity";[1]
let it poison the poison of every demon,
let it expel every impure spirit
and drive away every wicked spirit;
let it eradicate every fever,
all shivering and weakness;
let it procure good grace and remission of sins,
remedy of life and salvation, health and wholeness
of soul, body and spirit
and full vitality.

Let every satanic power, Lord,
every demon, every plot of the Adversary,
every plague and every torment,
every suffering and every pain,
every blow, shock and shadow,
dread thy holy name
that we now invoke,
and the name of thine only-begotten Son.
Let them depart from thy servants
inwardly and outwardly,
so that his name may be sanctified
who was crucified for us,
who rose from the dead,
who "bore our diseases and our infirmities",[2]

---

[1] Mt. 4, 23; 9, 35; 10, 1.
[2] Mt. 8, 17.

Jesus Christ, who is to come
"to judge the living and the dead".[1]

Through him, glory to thee and power,
in the Holy Spirit,
now and for ever and ever.
     Amen.


## 30. Prayer for a dead man or woman

O God who hast power over life and death,
"God of spirits and Lord of all flesh",[2]
God who givest death and life,
who "leadest to the gates of hell
and dost bring back from there":[3]

Thou dost create the spirit of man in him;
thou dost gather and give rest to the souls of the saints;
thou dost change, transform
and transfigure thy creatures
according as it is just and profitable.
Thou alone art incorruptible, unchanging and eternal.

We pray to thee for the sleep
and the repose of this man thy servant
          (or: this woman thy servant).
Refresh his soul and his spirit
in the places of pasture, the dwellings of repose,[4]
with Abraham, Isaac, Jacob and all the saints.

---

[1] I Tim. 1, 17.
[2] Num. 16, 22.
[3] Wisdom 16, 13.
[4] An allusion to Ps. 23, 2.

As for his body, do thou raise it
on the day thou hast appointed
according to thy sure promises.
Grant it, in thy holy pastures,
that part of the inheritance which belongs to it.

Do not be mindful of his faults and sins.
Grant that his death be peaceful and blessed.

Heal the sadness of those who live on
through thy consoling Spirit.
Grant to us all a happy end.

Through thine only-begotten Son, Jesus Christ.
Through him, glory to thee and power,
in the Holy Spirit,
for ever and ever.
    Amen.

# 7

# The Anaphora of Addai and Mari
### *(3rd or 5th century)*

# Introduction

The Chaldean Liturgy of the "holy apostles" Addai and Mari is the liturgy of the Uniate Chaldeans (Catholic) and of the Christians of Malabar in India.[1]

When analysed the anaphora of the mass allows one to uncover "a document of Syrian origin, for which there is no certain Greek prototype".[2] According to B. Botte,[3] the anaphora in its primitive form dates from the third century (and would therefore be contemporary with that of Hippolytus of Rome), the narrative of the Institution having subsequently dropped out. According to A. Raes on the contrary it dates only from the fifth century.[4]

## Acclamation

— The grace of our Lord Jesus Christ,
the love of God the Father
and the fellowship of the Holy Spirit
be with us all[5]
now and always
and for ever and ever.
— Amen.

---

[1] See V. Ermont, art. "Addée et Mari (liturgie d')" in *Dict. d'Archéologie chrétienne et de Liturgie*, vol. 1 (1907), col. 519–523.

[2] N. Maurice-Denis and R. Boulet, *Euchariste*, Paris, 1953, p. 301.

[3] B. Botte, "L'anaphore chaldéenne des apôtres" in *Orientalia christiana periodica*, 15 (1949), pp. 250–276.

[4] A. Raes, in *Lexikon für Theologie und Kirche*, vol. 6 (1961), 1089–1090.

[5] A phrase adapted from II Cor. 13, 14.

— Lift up your hearts.
— To thee, King of glory,
   God of Abraham, Isaac and Jacob.
— The oblation is offered to God,
   To the Lord of the universe.
— It is worthy and necessary.

## Preface

It is worthy that all mouths glorify,
that all tongues proclaim,
that all creatures adore and magnify
the adorable name of the glorious Trinity,[1]
of the Father, Son, and Holy Spirit.
He has created the world through his grace,
and in his kindness those who dwell in it.
He has saved men in his mercy,
he has granted to mortals the riches of his grace.

## Sanctus[2]

Thousands upon thousands of heavenly spirits
bless thee and adore thee.
Myriads upon myriads of the army
of servants of fire and spirit
sing thy name.
With the Cherubim and the Seraphim
they glorify and adore thy greatness.

---

[1] The words "of the glorious Trinity" are a later insertion into the primitive form of the text.

[2] The Sanctus is an addition to the primitive text.

They call ceaselessly
and reply one to another:

Holy, holy, holy is the Lord Sabaoth!
Heaven and earth are filled
with his splendour, his presence
and the brilliance of his greatness.
Hosanna to the highest heaven!
Hosanna to the Son of David!
Blessed be he who comes and is to come
in the name of the Lord.
Hosanna to the highest heaven!
And with the heavenly powers . . .


## Preface (continued)

We bless thee, Lord,
we thy servants, weak, feeble and infirm,
for the measureless grace that thou hast done us
for which we cannot repay thee.

Thou hast clothed thyself in our humanity,
to give us life through thy godhead.
Thou hast lifted up our lowliness,
thou hast restored our fall.
Thou hast raised up our mortality,
thou hast forgiven our faults,
thou hast justified us out of our sins.
Thou hast enlightened our understanding.
Thou hast condemned our enemies, Lord our God,
thou hast given triumph
to the frailty of our feeble nature,
through the abundant mercies of thy grace.

For all thy help and thy grace
we offer thee praise and blessing,
honour and adoration,
now and always
and for ever and ever.
Amen.

## *The account of the Institution*[1]

## *Anamnesis*

And we too thy servants,
weak, feeble and frail,
who are gathered in thy name,
we stand before thee at this time,
we have received from tradition
the symbolic rite which comes from thee.

With joy and exultation,
we give glory to thee,
we commemorate and accomplish
this great, fearful and holy,
life-giving and divine mystery
of the passion and the death,
the burial and the resurrection
of our Lord and our Saviour Jesus Christ.

---

[1] The recital of the Institution must be placed at this point in the anaphora. In the sixteenth century, the catholic Chaldeans re-introduced it into the text, in imitation of the Roman canon.

## Epiclesis

Let thy Holy Spirit, Lord, come
and rest upon this offering of thy servants,
let him bless it and sanctify it,
so that it may procure for us, Lord,
pardon for our offences and forgiveness of our sins,
the great hope of the resurrection of the dead,
and the new life in the kingdom of heaven
with all those who were pleasing to thee.

## Final doxology

For thy great and wonderful design
that thou hast realised in our regard,
we bless thee and glorify thee without end
in thy Church that thou hast redeemed
with the precious blood of thy Christ.
With open mouths and faces uncovered
we offer praise and glory,
blessing and adoration
to thy living, holy and life-giving name,
now and always,
and for ever and ever.
    Amen.

# 8

# The Strasburg Papyrus
*(4th-5th century)*

# *The Strasburg Papyrus*

The University Library at Strasburg preserves, under the number Gr 254, several much-mutilated fragments of papyrus which on examination prove to be part of the so-called alexandrian anaphora of St Mark.

The writing dates from the 4th-5th century. In their analysis of this document M. Andrieu and P. Collomp write: "Until now the liturgy of St Mark was known only through certain late manuscripts. Our manuscript is perhaps seven or eight centuries older. It is, in addition, itself only a copy, already altered, and the text which it contains goes back even earlier. It would not be rash to affirm that this version of the anaphora of St Mark was already circulating in the time of St Athanasius."[1]

## *Preface*[2]

*It is truly worthy and just*
*to sing thee and celebrate thee,*
to bless thee *and to adore thee* day and night . . .

*Thou hast created the heavens* and all that they con*tain,*
*the earth and all that it encloses,*
the sea and the riv*ers and all that people them.*
Thou hast created man *to* thine im*age* and likeness.
Thou hast created the universe through thy wisdom,
thy true Light,
thy Son Jesus Christ,

---

[1] *Revue des Sciences religieuses* (Strasburg), 8 (1928), p. 514.
[2] The passages in italic type represent a conjectural restoration based on more recent documents.

our Lord and Sav*iour*.
Through him and with him
and with the Holy Spirit
we offer thee in thanksgiving
this spiritual oblation,
this bloodless sacrifice,
that all peoples offer thee,
from the rising of the sun to its setting, from north to south,
for thy name is great among the nations
and in every place they offer incense to thy holy name,
a pure offering,[1]
a sacrifice and an oblation . . .


## Prayer of intercession

We pray and beseech thee:

Be mindful of thy Church, one, holy and catholic, of all peoples
    and of all thy fold.

Confirm in all our hearts the peace which comes from heaven;
    but give us also, according to thy grace, peace in this *life*.

Give to the *king* of the earth (to keep in his heart) thoughts of
    peace towards us and towards thy holy name . . .

*We pray thee, Lord, to keep the fruits of the earth for the sewing and the*
    harvest, for the sake of the poor among *thy peo*ple, for the
    sake of all of us who call upon *thy* name, of all those who
    hope in thee.

------------

[1] An adaptation of Mal. 1, 11.

(Be mindful) of those who have fallen asleep. Give rest to their
    souls.

Be mindful of those whom we call to mind today, of those whose
    names we *call* out, as also of those whom we do not name . . .

(Be mindful) of our *holy* fathers and of the bishops everywhere
    who profess the true faith.

Grant us to have part and inheritance . . . in the glorious com-
    munity of thy holy prophets, apostles and martyrs (. . .)[1]

> Through our Lord and Saviour.
> Through him, glory to thee,
> for ever and ever.
>     *Amen.*

---

[1] The four following lines are illegible.

# 9

# The Apostolic Constitutions
*(about 380)*

# The Apostolic Constitutions

The *Apostolic Constitutions* represent the largest liturgical-canonical compilation of antiquity. It purports to give the decrees which Pope Clement of Rome[1] received from the Apostles and sent out "to the bishops and priests". In fact the work is apocryphal. The author has made use of documents that were already in existence and ascribed his work to Clement in order to give it greater authority.

In Books I—VI he has used the *Didascalia of the Apostles*[2] as his source.

Book VII divides into two parts. The first is an expansion of the *Didache*;[3] the second a euchology grouping together some ancient prayers.

Book VIII is derived from the *Apostolic Tradition* of Hippolytus of Rome.[4] It contains liturgical formulas for ordinations. This is the most interesting part of the whole collection, for the author, in describing the ceremonies of the consecration of a bishop, has also inserted the prayers of the mass, the so-called Clementine Liturgy.

The work saw the light of day about 380 in Syria or at Constantinople.

The orthodoxy of the author is not entirely above suspicion. Some of his formulas are tinged with Arianism. For this reason the work was condemned at the Council *In Trullo* (691–692) as "falsified by heretics" and has exerted no marked influence in the history of the Church. However, if these "falsifications", which are easy to recognise, are omitted, the work remains a valuable witness to the liturgy of the fourth century.

Here I have used principally the prayers of the euchology[5] in Book VII and the liturgy of the "Clementine" mass[6] from Book VIII.

---

[1] On Clement of Rome, see *Les Pères apostoliques* (Vivante Tradition), p. 22.
[2] See pp. 77–96.
[3] See *Les Pères apostoliques*, op. cit., pp. 12–19.
[4] See pp. 29–73.
[5] See pp. 152–161.
[6] See pp. 161–183.

*Prayers*

# The Lord's Day

On the day of the Resurrection of the Lord, which we call
the Lord's day, you must always gather together to give thanks[1]
to God and to bless him for all the benefits with which he has
loaded us through Christ, in rescuing us from the bonds of
ignorance and error.

Let your sacrifice be spotless and pleasing to God, who has
said of his ecumenical Church:[2]

> In every place I am offered
> incense and a pure offering.
> For I am a great king,
> says the Lord Almighty,
> and my name is wonderful among the nations.[3]

> (VII, 30, 1–2.)

# Our eternal Saviour

> Our eternal Saviour and King of gods,
> who alone art all-powerful and Lord,
> God of the whole universe,[4]
> God of our holy and spotless fathers
> who have gone before us,
> God of Abraham, Isaac and Jacob,
> merciful and compassionate,
> patient and rich in mercies:[5]

---

[1] The word used (*eucharistein*) signifies the celebration of the eucharist, which is
pre-eminently the Church's sacrifice of thanksgiving.

[2] I.e., universal Church.

[3] Mal. 1, 11, 14.

[4] Esther 4, 17.

[5] Ex. 34, 6–7; Joel 2, 13.

Before thee, every heart is bared
and every secret thought is uncovered.
The souls of the just cry out to thee,
in thee the saints hope and trust.


Father of those who are without reproach,
thou listenest to those who call on thee uprightly,
thou hearest even silent appeals.
Thy providence indeed reaches
even to the heart of man
and thy knowledge searches
the mind of each.
In every region of the earth,
the incense of prayers and supplications
rises towards thee.


Thou hast made this world an arena
(where we struggle) for righteousness;[1]
but thou hast opened the gate of mercy to all.
Thou hast shown to every man,
by inborn knowledge and natural judgment
and by the proclamation of the Law,
that the possession of riches is not eternal,
that the splendour of beauty does not last,
that physical strength vanishes away,
that everything is vapour and emptiness.[2]


All that abides is the consciousness of a pure faith.
With the truth it penetrates

---

[1] An allusion to I Cor. 9, 24-25, where Paul compares Christian life to a race in the stadium.

[2] Eccles. 1, 3.

even to the very height of heaven
and takes possession of the joys to be.
Even before it has received,
thanks to the resurrection,
the promise of a new birth,
the soul exults in the joy of hope.

For, from the beginning, when our father Abraham
undertook to walk in the way of truth,
thou didst reveal thyself to him and guide him,
thou didst teach him the true nature of the present age.
His faith preceded his knowledge,
and the Covenant accompanied his faith.
For thou didst tell him:
"I will multiply thy descendants
like the stars in heaven,
like the sand on the sea-shore".[1]

So too, in giving him Isaac
whose life, according to thy designs,
was to be like to his own,
thou didst proclaim thyself his God, saying:
"I will be thy God
and the God of thy descendants after thee".[2]

So too again, when our father Jacob
set out for Mesopotamia,
thou didst tell him, showing him the Messiah:
"Behold, I am with thee.
I will increase and multiply thy posterity".[3]

---

[1] Gen. 13, 16.
[2] Gen. 17, 7; 26, 3.
[3] Gen. 48, 4.

To Moses also, thy faithful servant,
thou didst say, in the vision of the bush:
"I am who I am.
Such is my name which is to be remembered
by generation after generation".[1]

Defender of the descendants of Abraham,
blessed be thou through the ages.

(VII, 33, 2–7.)


## We give thee thanks

We give thee thanks, almighty Lord,
for all thy benefits.
Thou hast not removed from us
thy kindnesses and thy mercies,
but thou dost save from generation to generation,
thou dost deliver, thou dost come to our help
and thou dost protect (. . .)

For all thy benefits, to thee, (Father),
glory and veneration,
through Jesus Christ,
now and always and for ever.
Amen.

(VII, 37, 1 and 8.)


## Profession of faith for future neophytes

I believe and I have been baptised,

In the one, the uncreated,[2] the only true God almighty,
Father of Christ,

---

[1] Ex. 3, 14–15.
[2] Literally: not begotten, *agennetos*: see p. 104, n. 1.

who created and made all things and "from whom all things come",[1]

And in Jesus Christ the Lord, his only-begotten Son, "first-born of every creature",

who was begotten, not created, before the ages, according to the Father's good pleasure,

"through whom all things were made",[2] those in heaven and those on earth, the visible and the invisible,

who, in the last times, came down from heaven, was incarnate and was born of Mary, the holy virgin,

who lived a holy life according to the law of his God and Father,

who suffered under Pontius Pilate and died for us,

who, after his passion, was raised from the dead on the third day,

who ascended into heaven and sits at the right hand of the Father,

who will come again with glory at the consummation of the age, to judge the living and the dead, whose kingdom has no end.[3]

I have been baptised also in the Holy Spirit, the Paraclete, who assists all the saints from the beginning of the world,

whom the Father sent to the Apostles, according to the promise of our Saviour and Lord Jesus Christ,

whom he has sent since then to all those who believe in the holy, catholic and apostolic Church,

and in the resurrection of the flesh,

in the forgiveness of sins,

in the Kingdom of heaven and in the life of the age to come.

(VII, 41, 4–8.)

---

[1] Col. 1, 15.
[2] I Cor. 8, 6.
[3] A borrowing from II Tim. 4, 1 and Lk. 1, 33.

## Confirmation[1]

## *Prayer of anointing*

When (the bishop) has administered baptism in the name of the Father, Son and Holy Spirit, he gives (the neophyte) an anointing with oil. He is to say:

> Lord God, uncreated and without equal,
> Lord of all things,
> who hast diffused among all nations
> the sweet fragrance of the knowledge of the Gospel:
> let this oil be effective for the one baptised;
> through it, let the fragrance of Christ
> abide in him firm and stable;
> let it raise and give life
> to him who dies with Christ.

> (VII, 44, 1–2.)

## *The Our Father*

After that, (the neophyte) is to stand up and say the prayer the Lord taught us.

> (VII, 45, 1.)

## *Ritual of prayer*

It is right that he who is risen[2] should stand upright to pray, for when one is risen one stands upright. He who has died and risen with Christ is therefore to stand upright.

---

[1] As in the *Apostolic Tradition* (see p. 60), the rite of confirmation follows immediately on that of baptism.

[2] I.e., the baptised.

He is to turn to the East when he prays. For this is written in the second book of Chronicles: when Solomon had finished building the temple of the Lord, at the Dedication, the priests, the levites and the singers, with cymbals and harps, turned to the East, praising, blessing and singing:

> Praise the Lord, for he is good,
> for his mercy is everlasting.[1]

(VII, 45, 1–2.)

## Prayer of the one confirmed

After the first prayer, he is to say:

> Almighty God,
> Father of thy Christ, thine only-begotten Son,
> give me a spotless body, a pure heart,
> a watchful spirit, a knowledge without error.
> Let the Holy Spirit come
> so that I may possess the truth and believe it firmly,
> through thy Christ.
>
> Through him, glory to thee, in the Holy Spirit,
> for ever.
>     Amen.

(VII, 45, 3.)

---

[1] II Chr. 5, 12–13. The author has manipulated the text, which in fact says merely that the levitical singers stood "on the eastern side of the altar". However, the orientation of the act of prayer is traditional in the first centuries (see p. 88, n. 2).

Hymns and Blessings

# Morning prayer[1]

Glory to God in the highest heaven
and peace on earth to men whom he loves.[2]

We sing thee, we bless thee,
we adore thee, we glorify thee,
we give thee thanks for thy measureless glory.

Lord God, King of heaven, God the Father almighty.
Lord the only-begotten Son, Jesus Christ,
and Holy Spirit.

Lord God, Lamb of God, Son of the Father,
thou who takest away the sins of the world,
have pity on us.
Thou who takest away the sins of the world,
receive our prayer.
Thou who sittest at the right hand of the Father,
have pity on us.

For thou alone art the Holy,
thou alone the Lord,

---

[1] This hymn, the *Gloria* of the Roman mass, is translated here not from the text of the *Apostolic Constitutions* which appears to have been influenced by the theology of the author, but from that of the *Codex Alexandrinus* which seems to represent the earliest version. (The text is to be found in F. X. Funk, *Didascalia*, op. cit., vol. 1, pp. 455 f.) The hymn was originally part of the morning office, according to the evidence of St Athanasius (*On Virginity*, ch. 20), and found its way into the liturgy of the mass about the beginning of the sixth century (see J.-A. Jungmann, *Missarum solemnia*, op. cit., vol. 2, pp. 103–118; M. Denis-Boulet, *Analyse des rites et prières de la messe* in A. G. Martimort, *L'Église en prière*, Desclée, 1961, pp. 335–337; J. Brinktrine, *Die heilige Messe*, Paderborn, 1950, pp. 75–82.

[2] Lk. 2, 14; for the meaning, see *Hymnes et prières* (Vivante Tradition), vol. 2, p. 91, note 1.

thou alone the Most High, Jesus Christ,
to the glory of God the Father.
  Amen.

(VII, 7, 47, 1–3.)

## Evening prayer

Children, praise the Lord,
praise the name of the Lord.

We praise thee,
we celebrate thee with hymns,
we bless thee for thy measureless glory,
Lord King, Father of Christ,
the spotless lamb who takes away the sin of the world.

To thee praise,
to thee hymns,
to thee glory,
God and Father,
through the Son, in the Holy Spirit,
for ever and ever.
  Amen.

Now let thy servant depart,
according to thy word, O Master, in peace.
For my eyes have seen thy salvation
that thou hast prepared before the face of the peoples.
Light to enlighten the nations
and glory of thy people Israel.

(VII, 48, 1, 4.)

---

[1] This evening prayer is made up chiefly from Ps. 113, 1, from the hymns *Gloria in excelsis* and *Te decet laus*, as well as the Song of Simeon, Lk. 2, 29–32.

## Blessing for a meal

> Blessed be thou, Lord,
> who hast fed me since my youth
> and dost give nourishment to all flesh.
>
> Fill our hearts with joy and gladness
> that we may always have what is necessary
> and abound in all good works,[1]
> in Christ Jesus, our Lord.
>
> Through him, glory to thee,
> honour and power, for ever.
> > Amen.

> > > > > > (VII, 49.)

# The Liturgy of the Mass

### The Liturgy of the catechumens[2]

## Litany for the catechumens

> Let the deacon invite the catechumens to prayer.

> All the faithful then pray for them whole-heartedly saying: "Kyrie eleison". Let the deacon pray for them like this:

Let us all pray fervently for the catechumens.

May he who is good and who loves men listen graciously to their

---

[1] A scriptural mosaic composed of phrases from Ps. 119, 12; Ps. 136, 25; Acts 14, 17; and II Cor. 9, 8.

[2] The prayers of this first part were said after the readings.

prayers and supplications, may he accede to their requests and give them his help, may he grant the desire of their heart, for their good.

May he reveal the Gospel of his Christ to them, may he enlighten them and strengthen them, may he instruct them in his divine knowledge.

May he teach them his laws and his commandments, may he fill them with his pure and salutary fear.

May he open the ears of their heart, so that they may meditate on his law day and night.

May he strengthen them in devotion, may he unite and gather them into his holy flock.

May he judge them worthy of the bath of the new birth, of the garment of immortality and of true life.

May he rescue them from all wickedness, may the Adversary be unable to attack them, "may he cleanse them flesh and spirit from all defilement".[1]

"May he dwell and walk in the midst of them"[2] through his Christ, "may he bless their coming in and their going out",[3] may he bring all their designs to completion for their good.

Let us again beg fervently that they may obtain forgiveness of their sins and through the initiation of baptism become worthy of the holy mysteries and the community of the saints.

Rise, catechumens. Ask peace of God through his Christ: that your day, as well as your life, may be filled with this peace and

---

[1] II Cor. 7, 1.
[2] II Cor. 6, 16.
[3] Ps. 121, 8; 90, 17.

remain sheltered from sin. (Ask for) a Christian death, for the mercy and kindness of God, for forgiveness of sins. Recommend yourselves to the only uncreated God, through his Christ. Bow down and receive the blessing.

To all these petitions which the deacon announces, let the people, especially the children, reply "Kyrie eleison" as we have already said.

(VIII, 6, 3–9.)

## Blessing of the catechumens

While the catechumens bow their heads the bishop pronounces this blessing over them:

Almighty God, uncreated and unapproachable,
thou the only true God,
God and Father of thy Christ, thine only-begotten Son,
God of the Paraclete and Lord of all things,
who hast appointed thy disciples
teachers of the instruction of truth:
Cast thine eyes now on thy servants
who are being instructed in the Gospel of thy Christ.

Give them "a new heart,
renew a right spirit in their breast",[1]
so that they may know thee
and may do thy will
"with their whole heart and willingly".[2]

[1] Ps. 51, 12.
[2] II Macc. 1, 3.

Make them worthy of the holy initiation,
join them to thy holy Church,
grant them to share in thy divine mysteries,
through Jesus Christ, our hope,
who died for them.

Through him, glory to thee and adoration,
in the Holy Spirit, for ever.
    Amen.

(VIII, 6, 10–13.)


## Dismissal of the catechumens

After that, the deacon is to say: "Catechumens, go in peace".
(VIII, 6, 14.)


### Litany for the faithful[1]

The deacon again says: Let no one come near who does not
have the right. Let us all, the faithful, kneel. Let us pray to God
through his Christ; let all of us beseech God fervently through
his Christ.

Let us pray for the peace and tranquillity of the world and the
holy churches. May the God of all things grant us firm and
lasting peace, may he make us to persevere and keep us in
the fullness of virtue and devotion.

---

[1] After the intercessory prayer for the catechumens, the community prays
again for "demoniacs" and those who were considered as such (*Apostolic
Constitutions*, VIII, 7), for the future neophytes (VIII, 8), for those who were
undergoing public penance (VIII, 9), and finally for the faithful themselves
VIII, 10).

Let us pray for the holy, catholic and apostolic Church, spread from one end of the world to the other. May God keep her sheltered from the disturbance and agitation of the waves, may he protect (this Church) founded on the rock, even to the end of the world.

Let us pray for this holy parish. May the God of all things judge us worthy to keep firm possession of his heavenly hope and to render him a constant tribute of prayer.

Let us pray for the episcopate of those who, throughout the world,[1] "rightly dispense the word of truth"[2] (. . .)[3] May the God of mercies, for the sake of their holy churches, keep them in health and honour, may he grant them long life and an honourable age, in piety and righteousness.

Let us pray too for our priests. May God preserve them from all shame and evil, may he grant them an upright and honourable priesthood.

Let us pray for all deacons and ministers of Christ. May God give them to serve him without fault.

Let us pray for the readers, singers, virgins, widows and orphans, for those who are married and their children. May God take pity on them all.

Let us pray for those who practise a holy continence. Let us pray for those who lead a life of chastity and devotion.

Let us pray for those who in the holy Church present offerings and give alms to the poor.

---

[1] Literally: under heaven.
[2] II Tim. 2, 15.
[3] The text here mentions by name the bishops Clement, Evodius and Annianus and their parishes.

Let us pray for those who bring oblations and first-fruits to the Lord our God. May the most good God reward them with his heavenly graces, may he give them a hundredfold in this world and eternal life in the world to come, eternal goods for temporal ones, heavenly goods for earthly ones.

Let us pray for our brothers who have recently received baptism. May God establish and strengthen them.

Let us pray for our brothers who are afflicted by sickness. May the Lord deliver them from all weakness and all infirmity, may he bring them back to his holy Church sound and safe.

Let us pray for those who are travelling by land or sea, for those who are condemned to the mines, to exile, to prison and fetters, for the sake of the name of the Lord. Let us pray for those who are subjected to an oppressive slavery.

Let us pray for our enemies. Let us pray for those who hate and persecute us for the sake of the name of the Lord. May God appease their fury and dissipate their hatred for us.

Let us pray for those who are outside (the Church) and astray. May the Lord convert them.

Let us remember the children in the Church. May the Lord give them a perfect fear and lead them to maturity.

Let us pray for one another. May the Lord keep us by his grace, may he protect us even to the end, may he "deliver us from evil",[1] and from "all the snares of those who do evil";[2] may he save us and bring us into his heavenly Kingdom.

Let us pray for every Christian soul.

---

[1] Mt. 6, 13.
[2] Ps. 141, 9.

In thy mercy, save us and deliver us, O God.

Let us rise. Let us pray fervently for one another and recommend ourselves to the living God through his Christ.

(VIII, 10, 1–22.)

*Prayer of the bishop for the faithful*

After this the bishop says the following prayer:

Almighty Lord,
thou the Most High who dwellest in the highest heaven,
the Holy One who abidest in the midst of the saints,[1]
who art without beginning, who alone art Lord,
who hast given us through Christ the message
that makes known to us thy glory and thy name,
revealed by him to our understanding:[2]

Through him, cast now thine eyes
upon thy flock here.
Deliver them from all ignorance and sin,
give them to be filled with fear of thee,[3]
to love thee with love,
to worship the face of thy glory.

Be kind and gracious towards them,
hear their prayers,
keep them in an unchangeable steadiness,

---

[1] Is. 57, 15, quoted according to the Septuagint.
[2] The text here is muddled. It reads literally: "Through Christ, thou hast given us the message of the knowledge, for a profound knowledge of thy glory and thy name, that he has manifested to us for understanding".
[3] Literally: to fear thee with fear.

so that they may be holy in body and soul,
"without spot or wrinkle or any such thing".[1]
Let them be well disposed,
let none of them be weak or imperfect.


Mighty defender, who dost not accept persons,
come to the help of thy people here.
Thou hast chosen them from ten thousand,
thou hast redeemed them with the precious blood of thy
    Christ.
Thou art Master, helper, protector,
guardian, a sure rampart and a strong citadel,
for "no one can snatch anything from thy hand".[2]
There is no other god like thee;
"it is on thee that our hope rests".[3]


"Sanctify them in the truth,
for thy word is truth",[4]
thou who art beyond all injustice,
beyond all error.
Deliver them from every weakness and every infirmity,
from every fault, from all calumny and error,
"from fear of the enemy,
from the arrow that flies by day,
from the pestilence that walks in darkness".[5]
Judge them worthy of eternal life
which is in thy Christ, thine only-begotten Son,
our God and Saviour.

---

[1] Eph. 5, 27.

[2] Jn. 10, 29.

[3] Is. 45, 5; Ps. 62, 6.

[4] Jn. 17, 17.

[5] Ps. 91, 5–6.

Through him glory to thee and worship,
in the Holy Spirit,
now and for ever and ever.
    Amen.

(VIII, 11, 1-6.)

### Second Part: The Celebration of the Eucharist

# The kiss of peace[1]

Next the deacon says: Let us all attend.

The bishop then greets the assembly saying: The peace of
God be with you all.

The people reply: And with thy spirit.

The deacon says to all: Greet one another with a holy kiss.[2]

The clergy then give the kiss (of peace) to the bishop,
laymen give it to laymen, and women to women.

(VIII, 11, 7-9.)

### The Anaphora

# Acclamation

The bishop then begins the prayer, standing in front of the
altar: he is surrounded by the priests and splendidly adorned.

---

[1] As in the Catechetical Lectures of Saint Cyril of Jerusalem (*Mystagogical
Catechesis* 5; P.G. 33, 1109–1113), the kiss of peace is given before the anaphora.
In the West on the contrary it was placed after the Pater, as Saint Augustine witnesses
(*Sermon* 227; P.L. 38, 1101). The arrangement in use in the East seems to be the
more ancient.

[2] This formula is borrowed from the Pauline epistles, Rom. 16, 16, I Cor.
6, 20 and II Cor. 13, 12.

With his hand he signs his forehead with the triumphant sign of the cross and says: "The grace of almighty God, the love of our Lord Jesus Christ and the communion of the Holy Spirit be with you all."[1]

> With one voice all reply: "And with thy spirit".
>
> Then the bishop: "Let us raise our spirits".
>
> All: "They are turned to the Lord".
>
> The bishop: "Let us give thanks to the Lord".
>
> All the assembly: "It is worthy and just".
>
> (VIII, 12, 4–5.)

## Thanksgiving

The bishop continues: It is worthy and just to praise thee first of all, thee the one true God who dost exist before creation, from whom "all fatherhood in heaven and on earth has its origin"[2] (. . .) For all these benefits we give glory to thee, almighty God.

> (VIII, 12, 6 and 27.)

## Sanctus

It is thou who art adored by the numberless companies of Angels, Archangels, Thrones, Dominions, Principalities, Powers

---

[1] This trinitarian blessing is inspired by II Cor. 13, 13.

[2] Eph. 3, 15. Here a very long prayer has been omitted: it recalls the principal benefits of creation and of the history of the chosen people and it seems to derive its inspiration from the Jewish liturgy of Yom Kippur (see L. Ligier, *Péché d'Adam et péché du monde. Bible Kippur. Eucharistie*, Paris, 1961, vol. i, pp. 289–307).

and Virtues, of the hosts of eternity, as well as the Cherubim and the Seraphim with six wings, two to cover their feet, two to veil the head and two with which to fly. With the thousand thousand Archangels and the myriad on myriad of Angels, they sing unceasingly,—and let all the people say with them:

> Holy, holy, holy
> is the Lord Sabaoth.
> Heaven and earth are filled with his glory.
> Blessed is he for ever.     Amen.[1]
>
> (VIII, 12, 27.)

## The account of the Institution

Then the bishop continues:

> Thou art truly holy, most holy,
> Most High, exalted for ever.
>
> Holy too is thine only-begotten Son,
> our Lord and God, Jesus Christ (. . .)
> He was born of the Virgin,
> he took flesh, he who is God and Word,
> well-beloved Son, "first-born of every creature".[2]
> According to the prophecies made of him,
> he came of the stock of David and Abraham,
> of the tribe of Judah (. . .)

---

[1] Is. 6, 2–3; Dan. 3, 28.
[2] Col. 1, 15.

He, the just judge, was given over to the governor Pilate,
he was condemned, he the Saviour.
He was fixed to the cross
though he ought not to have known suffering.
He died,
though he is immortal by nature.
He was buried,
though it is he who gives life,
to deliver his own[1] from suffering,
to rescue them from death,
to break the fetters of the devil
and free men from his deceit.

He rose from the dead on the third day,
dwelt among his disciples for forty days,
ascended into heaven
and sits at thy right hand, O God and Father.

We then, recalling the sufferings
which he endured for us,
give thee thanks, almighty God,
not as well as we ought,
but as well as we can,
and fulfil his last testament.

For, on the night when he was betrayed,
he took bread in his holy and spotless hands,
and, lifting his eyes to heaven
towards thee, God and Father,
he broke it and gave it to his disciples, saying:
"This is the mystery of the New Testament.

---

[1] Literally: those for whom he had come.

Take and eat of it:
This is my body which is broken for many
for the forgiveness of sins."

He also filled the cup with wine mixed with water,
blessed it and gave it to them, saying:
"Drink of this, all of you, this is my blood,
which is poured out for many
for the forgiveness of sins.
Do this in memory of me.
For each time that you eat this bread
and that you drink this cup,
you proclaim my death
until I return."

(VIII, 12, 28–31, 33, 37.)

## Anamnesis

Mindful then of his passion and death,
of his resurrection from among the dead,
of his return to heaven,
and of his second coming
when he will come with glory and power
to judge the living and the dead
and render to each according to his works,
we offer thee, O King and God,
according to his testament, this bread and this cup.
We give thee thanks through him
for having judged us worthy
to stand before thee
and exercise this priesthood for thee.

And we beg thee
to look down graciously
on these offerings which we bring thee,
O God, who hast need of nothing,
and to accept them as pleasing to thee,
in honour of thy Christ.

(VIII, 12, 38–39.)

## *Epiclesis*

Send down upon this sacrifice thy Holy Spirit,
"witness of the sufferings of the Lord Jesus",[1]
that he may make this bread
the Body of thy Christ,
and this cup
the blood of thy Christ.

May those who share in it
be strengthened in devotion,
obtain forgiveness of sins,
be delivered from the devil and his errors,
be filled with the Holy Spirit,
become worthy of thy Christ,
enter into possession of eternal life
and be reconciled with thee, almighty God.

(VIII, 12, 39.)

### *The bishop's litany*

We pray to thee, Lord, for thy holy Church, which stretches from
one end of the world to the other, "which thou hast obtained
by the precious blood"[2] of thy Christ. Keep her sheltered

---

[1] I Peter 5, 1.
[2] Acts 20, 28.

from the disturbance and agitation of the waves, even to the end of the world.

(We pray to thee) for the universal episcopate which "rightly dispenses the word of truth".[1]

We pray to thee for myself, the humble (celebrant) who presents the offering to thee, for the whole college of priests, for the deacons, for all the clergy. Teach them wisdom, fill them with the Holy Spirit.

We pray to thee, Lord, for the king, for those who hold authority, for the whole army. May we live in peace, may we pass our whole lives in tranquillity and harmony, glorifying thee through Jesus Christ, our hope.

We present the offering to thee for all the saints who have been pleasing to thee from the beginning, patriarchs, prophets, just men, apostles, martyrs, confessors, bishops, priests, deacons, subdeacons, readers, singers, virgins, widows, lay people, and for all those whose names thou knowest.

We present the offering to thee for thy people who are here, that they may become "a royal priesthood and a holy nation"[2] to the praise of thy Christ, for those who practise virginity and continence, for the widows of the Church, for those who live in a holy marriage and for their children, for the infants of thy people. Do not cast out anyone from among us.

We pray to thee for this city and for its inhabitants, for the sick, for those subjected to harsh slavery, for the exiled, for the proscribed, for travellers by sea and land. To all of them be succour, help and defence.

---

[1] 2 Tim. 2, 15.
[2] II Peter 2, 9.

We pray to thee for those "who hate and persecute us for the sake of thy name",[1] for those who are outside and straying. Lead them back to what is good and appease their fury.

We pray to thee for the catechumens of the Church, for those who are tormented by the Adversary, for our brothers who are undergoing penance. As for the first, strengthen them in the faith; as for the second, keep them from the attacks of the Evil One; as for the last, grant them, as to ourselves, forgiveness of sins.

We present the offering to thee for good weather and an abundant harvest. Enable us, who receive thy benefits unceasingly, always to praise thee, "who givest food to all flesh".[2]

We pray to thee too for those who are absent with good cause.

Keep us all in our devotion, gather us into the Kingdom of thy Christ, the God of every visible and rational creature, our King. Let us dwell unshaken, without fault or reproach.

For to thee, Father, Son and Holy Spirit, is all glory, worship, thanksgiving, honour and adoration, now and always, and to endless and everlasting ages without end.

Let all the people reply: Amen.

(VIII, 12, 40–51.)

### The deacon's litany

The bishop says: The peace of God be with you all.

All the people reply: And with thy spirit.

---

[1] Mt. 10, 22.

[2] Ps. 136, 25.

The deacon proclaims anew: Let us pray to God once again through his Christ.

Let us pray for the offering which we present to the Lord, our God. May God in his goodness accept it, through the mediation of his Christ, upon his heavenly altar as a sweet savour.

Let us pray for this church and for the people.

Let us pray for the universal episcopate, for the whole college of priests, for all the deacons and ministers of Christ, for all the assembly of the church. May God keep and protect them all.

Let us pray "for kings and for those who hold authority". May we dwell in peace, "that we may be able to lead a quiet and peaceful life, in all piety and worthiness".[1]

Let us remember the holy martyrs, that we may be judged worthy to have a share in their struggle.

Let us pray for those who have fallen asleep in the faith.

Let us pray for good weather and for the ripening of the fruit.

Let us pray for those who have recently been enlightened by baptism. May they be strengthened in the faith.

Let us pray earnestly for one another.

Deliver us, O God, through thy grace. Thus delivered, let us recommend ourselves to God through his Christ.

(VIII, 13, 1-9.)

---

[1] I Tim. 2, 1-2.

*Communion liturgy*

## Preparatory prayer

The bishop says:

> "Great God, whose name is sublime,
> who art magnificent in thy designs
> and powerful in thy works",[1]
> God and Father of Jesus,
> thy holy Son, our Saviour:
> Cast thine eyes upon us, upon thy people here,
> whom thou hast chosen through Christ,
> to the glory of thy name.
>
> Sanctify us body and soul,
> "cleanse us from all defilement
> of flesh and spirit".[2]
> Grant us the good things here present.
> Do not judge any among us unworthy,
> but be our help, succour and defence,
> through thy Christ.
>
> Glory, honour and praise,
> glorification and thanksgiving,
> to thee, as to the Son and the Holy Spirit,
> for ever.
>         Amen.

---

[1] Jer. 32, 18–19 (quoted in the Septuagint version, Jer. 39, 19).

[2] II Cor. 7, 1.

## Acclamation of the people

When everyone has replied: Amen, the deacon says: Attend.

The bishop then addresses the people in these words: "Holy things to the holy".

The people are to reply:

> One single Holy One, one single Lord,
> Jesus Christ, who is blessed for ever,
> to the glory of God the Father.   Amen.

> "Glory to God in the highest heaven,
> on earth, peace,
> among men, good will (of God)."[1]

> Hosanna to the Son of David.
> Blessed be he who comes in the name of the Lord.
> God the Lord has shown himself among us.
> "Hosanna in the highest heaven".[2]

## The rite of communion

The bishop then communicates, followed by the priests, the deacons, the subdeacons, the readers, the singers and the monks; then, among the women, the deaconesses, the virgins and the widows; then the children; then the rest of the people, in order, with reverence and devotion, without disturbance.

---

[1] Lk. 2, 14.
[2] Mt. 21, 9.

As he gives the oblation, the bishop says: The Body of the Lord.

He who receives it is to reply: Amen.

On his part, the deacon takes the cup and says as he gives it: The blood of Christ, the cup of life.

He who drinks is to respond: Amen.

While communion is going on, Psalm thirty-three is recited.[1]

When all the men and women have communicated, the deacons are to take what is left over and carry it to the sacristy.

(VIII, 13, 10–17.)


## Prayer after communion

When the psalmist has finished, the deacon is to say:

> Having received the precious body and blood of Christ, let us give thanks to him who has made us worthy to participate in his holy mysteries.

> Let us beg him that they be not our condemnation, but our salvation, the well-being of soul and body, the safeguard of devotion, the forgiveness of sins, the life of the world to come.

Let us rise. Through the grace of Christ, let us recommend ourselves to the uncreated God and to his Christ.

(VIII, 14, 1–3.)

---

[1] In the Septuagint numbering; Ps. 34 in the Hebrew.

*Prayer of thanksgiving*

The bishop is to say the prayer of thanksgiving:

Lord God almighty,
Father of thy Christ, thy blessed Son,
thou who hearest those who call on thee uprightly,
who dost recognise even the prayers we make in silence:

We give thee thanks for having judged us worthy
to participate in thy holy mysteries.
Thou hast granted them to us
to strengthen in us the certainty
of the good things we already know,
for the safeguard of devotion,
for the forgiveness of sins,
for the name of Christ has been invoked upon us
and we have made our dwelling near to thee.

Thou hast separated us from the company of the unjust,
join us to those who are consecrated to thee.
Strengthened in the truth by the coming of the Holy
     Spirit,
show us that which we do not know,
fill up our deficiencies,
confirm that which we know.

Preserve the priests blameless in thy service,
keep kings in peace,
magistrates in justice.
Give us favourable weather,
harvests in abundance.
Keep the world in thine almighty Providence,
pacify the nations who desire war,
convert those who are in error.

Sanctify thy people,
protect the virgins,
keep the married in fidelity,
confirm those who live in chastity,
help the little children to grow,
strengthen the neophytes,
teach the catechumens
and make them worthy of initiation.
Gather us all in the Kingdom of heaven,
in Christ Jesus our Lord.

Glory, honour and worship
to thee, to Christ and to the Holy Spirit,
for ever.   Amen.

(VIII, 15, 1–5.)

### Final blessing

Let the deacon say: Bow your heads before God, through
his Christ, and receive the blessing.

The bishop then prays in this way:

Almighty God, true and without compare (. . .)
God of thy people, who believe in Christ:
Be gracious, hear me for the sake of thy name,
and bless those who have bowed their heads.
"Grant them the requests of their hearts",[1]
those which are for their good,
do not cast any of them out of thy Kingdom.
Sanctify them, keep them, protect them, help them,
deliver them from the Adversary, from every enemy.
Watch over their dwellings,
"keep their coming in and their going out".[2]

---

[1] Ps. 37, 4.
[2] Ps. 121, 8.

Glory to thee, praise and splendour,
worship and adoration,
and to thy Son, Jesus Christ,
our Lord, God and King,
and to the Holy Spirit,
now and always,
and for ever and ever.
Amen.

(VIII, 15, 6–9.)

### Dismissal

The deacon says: Go in peace.

(VIII, 15, 10.)

## 10

The Euchology of Der Balyzeh

# The Euchology of Der Balyzeh

In 1907, at Der Balyzeh, or the monastery of Balyzeh, in the neighbourhood of Assiut in Upper Egypt, a number of papyrus fragments written in Greek were found in the ruins of a Greek monastery destroyed more than a thousand years before. The scraps of papyrus were badly damaged, but when they were restored—often conjecturally—it was possible to recognise them as Christian prayers. It was generally admitted that they were liturgical texts of the ancient mass, including the remains of the prayer of intercession (*oratio fidelium*), the credo and the anaphora.[1]

Everything seemed to have been said on the subject of "the anaphora of Der Balyzeh" when it was all thrown into the melting pot again by the discovery of new fragments which made it possible to complete those already known.[2] The work revealed itself to be not so much a collection of specifically eucharistic prayers, but a more general one, a euchology. The three prayers "Thou, our help", "Give us charity" and "We pray to thee, O Master" are "prayers for all times". The *Credo* seems to come from a profession of faith at baptism like that found in the ritual of Hippolytus.[3] Lastly the anaphora does indeed give us the text of the ancient mass.

The papyrus itself dates from the sixth century, but the text preserves "some very ancient elements".[4] Across the centuries, the sparse remains of the Euchology of Der Balyzeh bring us an echo of the ancient prayer which once rose from distant Egypt to the Father of Jesus Christ, the "well-beloved Child".

---

[1] See for example P. Puniet, in *Revue Bénédictine*, 1909, p. 40; F. Cabrol, art. "Canon" in *D.A.C.L.* vol. 2 (1910), col. 1881–1895; H. Leclercq, art. "Messe" in *D.A.C.L.*, vol. 11 (1933), col. 624–626.

[2] These new fragments were published with the texts already known by C. H. Roberts and B. Capelle in "An early euchologium. The Der-Balyzeh Papyrus enlarged and re-edited" in *Le Muséon*, 23 (1949). It is the Greek text of this edition which has been followed here.

[3] See p. 58.

[4] Roberts and Capelle, op. cit., p. 52, prudently say: "A text which has preserved some very ancient elements but which as a whole can be regarded as a witness only for the time when the papyrus itself was written; about the end of the sixth century."

Note: In this translation the following conventions have been used. Italics represent a conjectual restoration of lacunae in the papyrus. Three continuous dots indicate a more important lacuna which it is impossible to restore.

### *Thou, our help*

. . .

Thou, our help.
Let not the pagans say:
"Where is their God?[1]
He has not saved them."
Thou, our help and our hope,
Thou, our refuge . . .
Thou, our protector!
Do not abandon us,
but rescue us from every danger
that threatens us,
and raise us on the great Day of the just.

Grant us to serve thee
through thy well-beloved Child,[2] Jesus Christ,
Through him, glory to thee, grace and honour,
*now* and for *generation* on generation,
*and for* ever and *ever*.
　　　Amen.

### *Give us charity*

. . .

May he give us charity and brotherly love
in the bond of peace.[3]

---

[1] Ps. 115, 2.
[2] See p. 14, n. 1,
[3] An allusion to Eph. 4, 3: "Strive to keep the unity of the spirit in *the bond of peace*."

May he hear the requests of our hearts,
he who alone holds power,
the holy Master,
shining with glory and honour,
whose name is Lord.

He dwells in the highest *heaven*
and casts his eyes upon the humble.
He is enthroned in the heavens.
He is blessed throughout the ages.
    Amen.

### *We pray to thee, O Master*

We pray to thee, O Master,
thou protector heavenly and sublime,
O God of truth
and Father of our Lord Jesus Christ,
who didst create the universe,
who dost contain all things
and alone cannot be contained,
who didst fix the bounds of heaven and earth,
the sea, the waves and the rivers,
the ebb and flow of the waves,
who didst take dust from the earth
and fashion man to thine image.
. . . *We pray thee,*
through Jesus Christ, our Lord,
thine only-begotten Son . . .
To thee, glory and power,
with thy *Holy* Sp*irit,*
*now and always,*
*and in* the ages *of eternity.*
    Amen.

*Profession of faith at baptism*

*The neophyte* proclaims the faith:

I believe in God, Father almighty,
in his only-begotten Son our Lord,
our Lord Jesus Christ,
in the Holy Spirit,
in the resurrection of the flesh,
*in the* holy catholic Church.

# Liturgy of the Mass

*Prayer of intercession*

*May* thy bless*ing come upon thy* people
*who do thy will.*[1]

Raise up those who have fallen,
Bring back those who have gone astray,
encourage those who are afraid.[2]

For thou art above every principality,
power, force and dominion,
above all that can be named
in this world and *in the world to come.*

---

[1] This fragment represents the end of the prayer of intercession.

[2] This passage is borrowed from the "Great Prayer" of Clement of Rome.
See *Les Pères apostoliques* (Vivante Tradition), p. 32.

*Anaphora*

## Preface

*Near to thee* stand
*the thousands of* holy *angels*
*and the* numberless *hosts of archangels.*
*Near to thee* stand
the Cherubim with many eyes.
Around thee stand the Seraphim,
each with six wings:
two to hide the face,
two to hide the feet,
two with which to fly.
Unceasingly they all acclaim thy holiness.
With all their acclamations of thy holiness,
receive also our acclamation
who sing to thee:

## Sanctus

Holy, holy, holy is the Lord,
the God Sabaoth.
Heaven and earth
are filled with thy glory.[1]

## Epiclesis[2]

Fill us too with thy glory.
And deign to send thy Holy Spirit

---

[1] Is. 6, 2–3.
[2] It is exceptional to find the epiclesis (see p. 40, n. 2.) placed before the consecration and for a long time this was thought to be the only example. However, in 1940, Lefort published an ancient anaphora showing the same peculiarity (*Le Muséon*, 1940, pp. 22–24).

on these offerings which thou hast created,
and make this bread to become
the body of our Lord and Saviour
Jesus Christ,
and this chalice to become
the blood of the New *Testament*
of our Lord, God and Saviour,
Jesus Christ.

## Prayer for the Church

*And as* this bread was scattered
on *the mountains*, the hills and in the valleys,
and was gathered to become a single body . . . [1]
as too this wine,
sprung from the *holy* vine of D*avid*,
and this water, sprung from the spotless Lamb,
were mixed
and became a single mystery,
so too do thou gather the catholic Church
of Jesus Christ.

## The account of the Institution

For our L*ord Jesus* Christ,
on the night when he *was betrayed*
*took bread in* his *holy hands*,
*gave* thanks and *blessed it*,
*sanctified and broke it*,
*gave it* to his dis*ciples and a*postles, saying:

---

[1] This passage is borrowed from the eucharistic prayer of the *Didache*, see p. 14.

"Take *and eat* of it, all of you.
This *is* my body
which is given for you
in forgiveness of sins."

Likewise, after the supper,
he took the chalice and blessed it,
drank of it and gave it to them, saying:
"Take, drink of it, all of you.
This is my blood
which is poured out for you
for the forgiveness of sins.
*Do this in memory of me*.

Each time that you eat this bread
and that you drink this chalice,
you announce my death,
you proclaim my resurrection,
*you make me*mory of me."

## Anamnesis

We announce thy death,
*we procl*aim thy Resurrection,
and we pray . . .
. . .

## Communion prayer

Give (thy servants)
the power of the Holy Spirit,
the confirmation and increase of faith,

the hope of eternal life to come,
through our Lord Jesus Christ.
Through him, glory to thee, Father,
with the Holy Spirit
for ever.
        Amen.

# Appendix: Roman Baptismal Inscriptions

## Baptistry of Saint Laurence in Damaso

From this noble spring a saving water gushes,
which cleanses all human defilement.

Do you wish to know the benefits of the sacred water?
These streams give the faith that regenerates.

Wash away the defilements of your past life in the sacred fountain.
Surpassing joy to share in the life the water brings!

Whoever resorts to this spring abandons earthly
things and tramples under foot the works of darkness.

## Baptistry of the Lateran

Here a people of godly race are born for heaven;
the Spirit gives them life in the fertile waters.
The Church-Mother, in these waves, bears her children
like virginal fruit she has conceived by the Holy Spirit.

Hope for the Kingdom of heaven, you who are reborn in this
spring,
for those who are born but once have no share in the life of
blessedness.
Here is to be found the source of life, which washes the whole
universe,
which gushed from the wound of Christ.

Sinner, plunge into the sacred fountain to wash away your sin.
The water receives the old man, and in his place makes the new
man to rise.

You wish to become innocent: cleanse yourself in this bath,
whatever your burden may be, Adam's sin or your own.

There is no difference between those who are reborn: they are one,
in a single baptism, a single Spirit, a single faith.
Let no one be afraid of the number or the weight of his sins:
He who is born of this stream will be made holy.

*Inscription of Sixtus III* (432–440)

### *Baptistry of Saint Laurence*

You who pass, consider how short life is.
Turn your vessel back towards the shores of Paradise,
return to port to look on the face of the Lord.
Accept grace, you who share in what is holy.

True God, supreme glory, light, wisdom and power:
from thy side, O wonderful might of thy love, thou pourest
both the blood, which on the altar appears like wine,
and the waters of baptism that purify souls.

(Fifth century.)

### *Inscription placed in the consignatorium*[1]

Here the innocent sheep, cleansed by the heavenly water,
are marked by the hand of the supreme Shepherd.

---

[1] The *consignatorium* was the place where the anointings of the newly baptised
were performed. Here without doubt it is the *consignatorium* of the Vatican basilica
which is meant.

You who have been begotten in this water, come to the unity
to which the Holy Spirit calls you, to receive his gifts.

You have received the cross: learn to escape the storms of the
  world:
that is the great lesson of which this place reminds you.[1]

---

[1] Possibly an allusion to the martyrdom of Saint Peter who according to
tradition was crucified here.

# Bibliography

## The Passover Meal and the Institution of the Eucharist in the New Testament

The text and notes are based on L. Deiss, *Synopse de Matthieu, Marc et Luc*, Desclée de Brouwer, Paris, 1963–1964.

For the ritual of the Jewish Passover, see L. Strack and P. Billerbeck, *Kommentar zum Neuen Testament*, Munich, vol. 4, 1st Part (3rd ed., 1961) pp. 41–76.

For the evolution of the Eucharist in the liturgy, see H. Leclercq, article "Messe" in the *Dictionnaire d'archéologie chrétienne et de liturgie*, vol. 11 (1933), col. 513–774; N. Maurice-Denis and R. Boulet, *Eucharistie ou la Messe dans ses variétés, son histoire et ses origines*, Paris, 1953; J. A. Jungmann, *Missarum Solemnia*, vol. 1, Paris, 1956; J. Lécuyer, *Le sacrifice de la Nouvelle Alliance*, Mappus, Le Puy, 1962; this study sets the Mass in the context of the Old and the New Testament better than any other.

## The Eucharistic Prayer of the Didache

At the moment the most thorough study of the Didache is that of J. P. Audet, *La Didachè, Instruction des Apôtres*, in the collection *Études Bibliques*, Gabalda, Paris, 1958. The text (and translation) of the eucharistic prayer: pp. 234–236.

## The Witness of Saint Justin

Christian initiation: *Apology* I, 61; *P.G.* 6, 420B–421B. The celebration of the Eucharist: *Apology* I, 65–66; *P.G.* 6, 428A–429A.

The Lord's day: *Apology* I, 67; *P.G.* 6, 430B–432A.

## The Apostolic Tradition of Hippolytus of Rome

— F. X. Funk, *Didascalia et Constitutiones Apostolorum*, vol. 2, *Testimonia et scripturae propinquae*, Paderborn, 1905, pp. 97–119. Funk gives the text of the old Latin translation, completed, where the Verona palimpsest is lacking, by a translation into Latin from the Coptic version. (The work of Funk has been re-issued by Bottega d'Erasmo, Turin, 1962.)

— R. H. Connolly, *The So-Called Egyptian Church Order and Derived Documents*, Cambridge, 1916 (Texts and Studies, VIII, 4). The text of the old Latin translation with an English translation based on the oriental versions where the old Latin is lacking.

— G. Dix, *The Treatise on the Apostolic Tradition of St Hippolytus of Rome, Historical Introduction, Textual Materials and Translation, with Apparatus Criticus and some Critical Notes*, London, 1937. The text of the old Latin translation with an English translation.

— B. Botte, *Hippolyte de Rome, la Tradition apostolique*, Sources chrétiennes 11, Paris, 1946. A French translation with the text of the old Latin version.

## The Didascalia of the Apostles

— P. A. De Lagarde, *Didascalia apostolorum syriace*, Leipzig, 1854. Syriac translation.

— E. Hauler, *Didascalia apostolorum fragmenta Veronensia Latina*, Leipzig, 1900. Fragments of the old Latin translation.

— F. X. Funk, *Didascalia et Constitutiones apostolorum*, vol. 1, Paderborn, 1905. The Greek text with Latin translation of the Apostolic Constitutions, Books I–VI: pp. 2–385.

— F. Nau, *La Didascalie, c'est-à-dire l'enseignement catholique des douze apôtres et des saints disciples de Notre Sauveur*, Paris, 1902; 2nd ed., 1912. French translation.

— H. Achelis and J. Flemming, *Die syrische Didaskalia übersetzt und erklärt*, in T.U., X, 2 (1904). A German translation which is closer to the original than the French one.

— R. H. Connolly, *Didascalia apostolorum. The Syriac Version translated and accompanied by the Verona Latin fragments*, Oxford, 1929.

A more complete bibliography is to be found in B. Altaner and H. Chirat, *Précis de patrologie*, pp. 98–99 and in J. Quasten, *Patrology*, Vol. 2, *The Ante-Nicene Literature after Irenaeus*, pp. 151 f.


## The Euchology of Serapion of Thmuis

— G. Wobbermin, in T.U. 17, 3b, 1898.

— F. X. Funk, *Didascalia et Constitutiones apostolorum*, vol. 2, pp. 158–195. Greek text with Latin translation.

# The Anaphora of Addai and Mari

— B. Botte, "L'Anaphore chaldéenne des apôtres" in *Orientalia christiana periodica*, 15, 3–4 (1949), pp. 250–276.

— A. Raes, "Le Récit de l'institution eucharistique" in *Orientalia christiana periodica*, 10, 1–2 (1944), pp. 216–226.

— G. Ratcliff, "The original form of the anaphora of Addai and Mari" in *Journal of Theological Studies*, 30 (1929), pp. 23–32.

# The Strasburg Papyrus

— Andrieu-Collomp, "Fragments sur papyrus de l'anaphore de S. Marc" in *Revue des sciences religieuses*, Strasburg, 8 (1928), pp. 489–515.

— F. E. Brightman, *Liturgies Eastern and Western*, vol. 1 (Oxford, 1896), pp. 115–143; 144–188.

# The Apostolic Constitutions

— F. X. Funk, *Didascalia et Constitutiones apostolorum*, vol. 1, Paderborn, 1905 (Turin, 1962), pp. 2–595. This critical edition by Funk replaces the edition in Migne, *P.G.* 1, 555–1156. For a bibliography of studies of the Apostolic Constitutions, see Altaner Chirat, *Précis de patrologie*, p. 101.

# The Euchology of Der Balyzeh

— T. Sermann, *Texte und Untersuchungen*, 35, 1.

— P. De Puniet, in *Revue Bénédictine*, 26 (1909), pp. 34–51.

— F. Cabrol, article "Canon" in *Dictionnaire d'Archéologie chrétienne et de liturgie*, 2 (1910), col. 1881–1891.

— C. Del Grande, *Liturgiae, preces, hymni christianorum e papyris collecti*, Naples, 2nd ed., 1934, 1–5.

— J. Quasten, *Monumenta eucharistica et liturgica vetustissima*, Bonn, 1935, pp. 37–44.

All these editions and studies have been rendered out of date by the discovery of new fragments belonging to the *Euchology of Der Balyzeh*, published by C. H. Roberts and B. Capelle, "An early euchologium. The Der Balyzeh Papyrus enlarged and re-edited" in *Le Muséon*, 23 (1949).

## *Appendix:* Four Roman Baptismal Inscriptions

The texts of these are to be found in Schuster, *Liber Sacramentorum*, vol. 1, p. 34: vol. 1, p. 32: vol. 8, p. 8: and vol. 1, p. 33.